"*Academically Speaking* offers a rich tou.
tion. Ostrander's ability to draw on a wide range of experiences as a student, professor, college administrator, consultant, and founding director of a Christian study offers insights and encouragement for anyone interested in understanding the landscape of higher education today."

—**Charlie Cotherman**, author of
*To Think Christianly: A History of L'Abri, Regent College,
and the Christian Study Center Movement*

"Embodying the posture of a teacher as storyteller, Ostrander weaves together his fascinating personal academic journey with historical and contemporary insights regarding trends in American higher education. The book will be a refreshing and engaging read for anyone who loves narratives about intellectual pilgrimage. Ostrander's vast array of roles and experiences in higher education also affords him a unique ability to speak insightfully about the strengths and struggles of both Christian higher education and Christians in higher education."

—**Perry Glanzer**, Baylor University

"With a historian's eye for seasons of change, *Academically Speaking* is a reflective memoir about Rick Ostrander's three decades in a network of faith-based colleges and their consortium partners. From the cadence of bike riding to his wife Lonnie's music lessons, Ostrander is a relational storyteller who values the spiritual formation of students in authentic community. A scholar and traditionalist at heart—yet futuristic and visionary in his optimism—Ostrander is one of our most important cultural translators and advocates for Christian higher education in the twenty-first century."

—**Karen An-hwei Lee**, Wheaton College

"For those whose Christian higher education careers have launched more recently, Ostrander's career journey will instruct and expand a vision of what this precious niche of American higher education has been and could be. The book shares pragmatic wisdom from an author with years of administrative experience, a background of professorial expertise, and a lifetime of Christian prayer and practice. The book's conclusion is worth the entire read, recommending that Christian colleges and universities offer authentic community as a salve to loneliness, a treasure with both mission integrity and market value in these immensely challenging times."

—**Jenell Paris**, Messiah University

"Reading *Academically Speaking* is like paging through a lovingly curated scrapbook of memories on the bookshelf labelled 'Christian higher education.' As a discerning guide and historian, Rick Ostrander brings candor and wit to the telling of his own story, one that remarkably weaves people and places significant to American evangelicalism around the turn of the twenty-first century. This book is especially poignant for Christian academics shaped by Mark Noll's *Scandal of the Evangelical Mind*—for we will recognize Ostrander's journey as our own."

—**Felicia Wu Song**, Westmont College

"*Academically Speaking* is an enlightening journey through Christian higher education in the United States. Rick Ostrander is a uniquely qualified guide to that journey, weaving a historian's insights into his own four-decade story of involvement with many of the people, institutions, and moments that have shaped the movement."

—**Noah Toly**, Calvin University

"Few educators can match Rick Ostrander for deep experience at an astoundingly wide range of universities and colleges, in both teaching and leadership. His candid and subtle memoir is a journey through some of the most interesting moments in the last half-century of Christian higher education; it's full of lessons on where Christian teachers, students and administrators have been, and where they're heading."

—**Molly Worthen**,
University of North Carolina at Chapel Hill

ACADEMICALLY SPEAKING

Lessons from a Life in Christian Higher Education

RICK OSTRANDER

WILLIAM B. EERDMANS PUBLISHING COMPANY
GRAND RAPIDS, MICHIGAN

Wm. B. Eerdmans Publishing Co.
4035 Park East Court SE, Grand Rapids, Michigan 49546
www.eerdmans.com

Published 2024

Book design by Lydia Hall

Printed in the United States of America

30 29 28 27 26 25 24   1 2 3 4 5 6 7

ISBN 978-0-8028-8339-1

Library of Congress Cataloging-in-Publication Data

A catalog record for this book is available from the Library
of Congress.

*To Lonnie, my companion, confidante,
and one true constant throughout life's journey*

Contents

CONTENTS

Foreword

I T MIGHT, AT FIRST GLANCE, seem presumptuous for someone still only in his fifties to write a memoir. Rick Ostrander's account of his career in evangelical Christian academia is, however, not first of all about himself, even though, inevitably, he is at the center of the story as participant, observer, and author. Rather, it is primarily an account of a fascinating journey in which the traveler describes highlights of what he encounters including the obstacles and twists and turns along the way. The traveler's perceptions are central aspects of the story, since what he encounters is refracted through his own personality, interests, and initiatives. Still, I think one can say of this story that it fits with the ideal that C. S. Lewis sets up for the poet. The poet, says Lewis, should not be saying, "Look at me." Rather the poet should be guiding our vision and saying, "Look at that."

The "that" in this case is the remarkable but often contested burgeoning of evangelical Christian intellectual life over the past forty years. The story that Rick has to tell is that of an insider who is in many ways representative of those developments. Forty years ago, when the story begins, he was about to enter Moody Bible Institute, long considered the informal headquarters of classic fundamentalism. But fundamentalism, which always had many sides, was changing in a number of ways. One sort of change was that some of its constituents were becoming less defensive in their engagement with the cultural mainstream. That was an era when conservative churches were growing, and one thing that meant was that they were becoming more suburban, affluent, and oriented to higher education. During the 1980s and 1990s many excellent evangelical students were entering graduate programs, especially those where there was some promise of sympathy with Christian commitments. Rick fit this pattern. After completing his collegiate studies at the University of Michigan, he enrolled in a PhD program to study American religious history at the University of Notre Dame.

It was there I had the pleasure of getting to know him and becoming his academic mentor. More importantly, I became good friends with him and with his personable and talented wife, Lonnie, and that valued friendship has continued since. I might add that one of the great pleasures in teaching students, especially at the graduate level, is that many of those students have become among my best friends, as is true in this case. Since then I have, of course, followed his career with interest, a good bit of which took place while we were both in Grand Rapids, Michigan, and in frequent contact.

After Notre Dame, Rick progressed through a variety of positions in Christian academic institutions, from history professor, to dean, to provost, to administrator in the Council for Christian Colleges and Universities (CCCU), to academic consultant, to special programs officer, and now as Executive Director of the Michigan Christian Study Center at the University of Michigan.

Rick's account of his journey, then, offers the reader an inside look at Christian higher education over the past generation. That has been an era of growth but also a time with many growing pains, and Rick's journey illustrates both. His observations, insights, and recommendations based on that journey will be of interest both to those inside the movement and to outside observers.

GEORGE M. MARSDEN
Francis A. McAnaney Professor of History Emeritus,
University of Notre Dame

Preface

THIS BOOK BEGAN AS a how-to manual on academic administration. Years ago, I wrote an introduction to Christian higher education for first-year college students, and so my original intention was to write something similar for new or aspiring academic administrators. I drafted a chapter with the alluring title "Supervising Personnel," based largely on my years as a provost, and had my wife look it over. "It's okay," Lonnie remarked, "but the interesting parts are your own experiences. Why don't you focus on those?" I'd written a few books over the years, but never a story, despite Lonnie's repeated encouragement to do so. The story that I know best is my own, so I dropped the instructional material and expanded the narrative, going all the way back to my first week in Bible college.

An autobiography about a life in academia isn't necessarily a page-turner, but this one might be more interesting than most, if for no other reason than its variety. My decades in higher education include a Bible college, a public university, a Catholic university, an emerging for-profit university, two evangelical universities, the Council for Christian Colleges & Universities, an educational technology company, a Christian liberal arts college, and finally a Christian study center. My roles at these organizations have included that of student, professor, administrator, consultant, salesperson, and entrepreneur. Finally, my story has included successes, unexpected failures, and attempts to discern God's leading and trust in his goodness amid times of uncertainty.

In the process of telling my own story, this book also narrates a larger story—the efforts by American Christians to institutionalize their commitment to loving God with their minds. Like me, Christian colleges and universities have experienced successes, failures, and hardships. Many of them face theological controversies; divisions between students, faculty, board members, and alumni; attacks from the left and from the right; and enrollment and financial challenges. Plenty of illustrative episodes appear in my narrative. Where such incidents involve existing people and institutions, I have sought to imitate my scholarly mentor, George Marsden, in combining honesty and generosity.

These institutions, however, also serve a vital purpose in cultivating graduates who make a difference in the world and providing a scholarly voice to counterbalance the anti-intellectualism that often emanates from evangelical populism. Moreover, Christian higher education has shown itself to be adaptable to changing conditions, and promising new approaches continue to emerge, such as the Christian study center movement. Such themes are woven throughout my story, and for readers wanting more reflection on Christian academia in general, the epilogue provides my perspective on and prescriptions for the future of Christian higher education.

My hope, therefore, is that the book appeals to three general audiences. First, current or prospective Christian higher-education professionals—whether faculty or staff—who toil away in a particular habitat will benefit from a look at the larger ecosystem. Furthermore, for Christians attempting to love God with both heart and mind and faithfully live out their particular calling, perhaps there's room in the literary world for another case study of a life of imperfect discipleship, containing at various times accomplishments, surprises, risks, and uncertainty. More generally, outsiders to Christian higher education can appreciate its importance to American political and cultural life in general, as the prominence of institutions such as Baylor University, Liberty University, and Wheaton College demonstrates. To such readers, this book hopefully will provide an engaging, informative window into an important subset of American higher education. Ultimately, if the number of readers who prefer a more general analysis of the state of Christian higher education is roughly equal to those who wish to see a more personal narrative, then I will have found the right balance.

Søren Kierkegaard once wrote, "Life can only be understood backwards, but it must be lived forwards." More personally, this memoir is an attempt to make sense of my life so far, and by doing so live forward more wisely. Perhaps those who read it might gain some wisdom for the living of their own lives, or at least greater insight into the strange and diverse world that is American Christian higher education.

ONE

Bible College Beginnings

I N THE LANDSCAPE of American higher education, Bible colleges are something of an anomaly. Founded by revivalists and missionaries in the late 1800s and early 1900s, they provided intensive, practical education to equip Christians for full-time ministry—typically understood as a pastor, evangelist, or missionary. In other words, Bible institutes were trade schools for Christian workers. The arts and sciences were unnecessary luxuries; instead, courses focused on the Bible, theology, evangelism, and practical ministry. Often these institutions were unaccredited and relied on the confidence of their constituents, which was often buttressed by the personal reputation of a prominent founder.

Over the course of the twentieth century, many Bible colleges either shut down or expanded their curriculum to include arts and sciences and evolved into degree-granting institutions. The Boston Missionary Training Institute, for example, eventually became Gordon College. The Bible Institute of Los Angeles cleverly converted its acronym into a university name, Biola. In the process, these institutions typically dropped "Bible" from their name but maintained a robust Bible curriculum to supplement majors in business, history, and the like.

One significant exception to this trend is the largest and most prominent of the Bible schools, Moody Bible Institute. Founded in downtown Chicago in 1886 and named after the prominent evangelist Dwight L. Moody, the school expanded throughout the course of the twentieth century. Its present-day campus occupies a significant portion of premier Near North Side real estate. And while it now offers accredited degrees, Moody has steadfastly maintained its name and identity as a Bible institute preparing students for full-time Christian service. As a result, Moody has retained a distinctive educational approach and subculture.

∞∞∞

It was at Moody Bible Institute that my academic journey began in the fall of 1984. This was before families planned their vacations around college visits, and for me, Moody, located thirty miles away from our home in suburban Chicago, was an easy choice. My father worked there as alumni director, my parents had attended Moody in the early 1960s, and my older sister was a current student. At the time, Moody did not offer four-year bachelor's degrees, so students who wanted to earn a degree attended for three years, then transferred to another institution for the final two years. My original plan was to attend Moody for one year to "get some Bible under my belt," then transfer to a four-year institution. In retrospect, that plan seems puzzling. While I grew up in the church and generally attended youth group, at least when it didn't conflict with sports obligations, I didn't plan to become a pastor or missionary and don't recall having an overwhelming interest in learning more about the Bible. Perhaps it was the allure of living in downtown Chicago, combined with an absence of clear goals steering me elsewhere, that led me to Moody.

I certainly had other options. I was fairly bright—A grades came easily to me, and I scored pretty high on the ACT and SAT. Also, I was a good high school shooting guard, and if I hadn't lost most of my junior season to a calf injury, probably would have received some modest scholarship offers from small colleges. Nevertheless, in late August 1984, I arrived at 820 North LaSalle Street for Welcome Week. At the time, Moody's student body was entirely undergraduate and overwhelmingly residential. Students arrived from all over the world, and the assumption was that they would live in one of the four main dormitory buildings. A smattering of off-campus married students did attend—typically, earnest young men with pastoral aspirations, clearly identified by their briefcases and sack lunches—but the typical student was an eighteen-to-twenty-year-old from Nebraska or a "missionary kid" from the Philippines who lived on campus.

Of course, living quarters were strictly segregated by sex, so there were two main dormitories for the men (Culbertson Hall and Dryer Hall) and two for the women (Houghton Hall and Smith Hall). To facilitate healthy interaction between the sexes, the school paired "brother" and "sister" floors. Members of these floors sat together in the dining room and occasionally held events together such as Christmas parties. Also, because this was downtown Chicago, if a female student needed to go shopping in the evening, she would contact someone from the brother floor to accompany her.

My floor, Culbertson 18, was paired with Houghton 9, and so at some point in Welcome Week, I met Lonnie Earhart, from Mount Joy, Pennsylvania. She was two years ahead of me in school, which made her a "senior" in Moody's three-year system, but had returned to campus early in order to help out with Welcome Week. Like me, Lonnie came from a "Moody" family; her mother had attended Moody, as had her two older brothers. She was an extrovert well known around campus, a talented singer, and an extraordinary pianist who could sight-read any score placed in front of her. She majored in sacred music and sang in the Moody Chorale. I don't remember our first meeting, but clearly we held enough mutual interest to begin spending time together. During one of our first evening walks around the city, I did my best to impress her. Unfortunately, my main sources for doing so were a vast knowledge of sports trivia and an ability to identify the expensive sports cars that drove by, neither of which made a positive impression.

Fortunately for me, Lonnie detected something deeper in me that was hidden beneath my vain, insecure, suburban high school jock exterior. I had always been a voracious reader, from sports books and *The Black Stallion* series as a grade schooler, to Lewis, Tolkien, London, and Tolstoy as a high schooler. Literature got me through many dull, unchallenging years of secondary school. In addition, I had a penchant for music that resonated with something deeper in me. At night in my bedroom, I would put on albums of Bach's *Brandenburg Concertos*, Tchaikovsky's *Swan Lake*, and most often, Gershwin's *Rhapsody in Blue* and listen to them in the dark. I had not yet read C. S. Lewis's *Surprised by Joy*, in which he describes being drawn toward God by an innate sense of longing, but these works of art were evoking something deep in me as well.

The relationship between Lonnie and me began platonically but received a boost from an unlikely source—the presidential election of 1984. Moody students held an election watch party in the dining room, which was decorated with red, white, and blue streamers and balloons. From the vantage point of today's hyperpoliticized evangelical culture, it's refreshing to recall how blissfully unpolitical and nonpartisan we Moody students were at the time. The election featured Ronald Reagan, darling of the recently formed Religious Right, against Walter Mondale, the liberal Democrat from Minnesota. And while Moody generally would have favored the stances of the former, the event was devoid of any partisan furor or a sense that the future of Christian civilization depended on Reagan's reelection. The important thing for me was that Lonnie wanted to stay for the balloon drop, but she had to leave early for a piano practice session. I stayed on until the end, corralled a balloon, and taped it to her mailbox on the first floor of Houghton. In thirty-six years of marriage, I have rarely surpassed that initial romantic act.

It took a while for the gallant balloon gesture to take effect, but by spring, Lonnie and I were clearly in a dating relationship. What that meant at a Bible college in the 1980s was complicated. Not surprisingly, Moody Bible Institute had plenty of rules, many of which related to relationships between male and female students. Visits between dormitories were strictly limited to "open dorm" hours on an occasional Friday evening. Of course, restrictions only strengthened the allure. Female students liked to sunbathe on the roof of Houghton Hall on Chicago's five warm sunny afternoons per year. Unfortunately the windows on the east end of Culbertson Hall overlooking Houghton were not only frosted but permanently locked, to the chagrin of the male residents. What romantic interactions that did exist often occurred in "prayer meetings" at the end of an evening date. The elaborate underground tunnel system that connected all of Moody's buildings provided a wealth of dark corners for couples to pray together and was regularly policed by resident assistants.

While dating was allowed, movies and alcohol were prohibited, and students had an 11:00 p.m. curfew on weeknights and midnight on weekends. Since most Moody students had little disposable income, movies and alcohol (not to mention dinners out) were generally inaccessible anyway. Instead, Chicago itself served as students' dating venue. Lonnie and I would walk down to Oak Street beach, or stroll the charming little side streets of the Gold Coast with names like Astor and Goethe and gaze into the windows of the brownstone houses at baby grand pianos, soft leather chairs, and chandeliers. Or we would hang out in the plush couches of the Ritz Carlton hotel lobby pretending to be customers, or splurge on a shared piece of cheesecake at Allie's Bakery on the seventh floor of the Marriott. Best of all, somehow word had spread among Moody students that the trap door leading to the roof of the forty-story Sheraton hotel was unlocked. While the Sheraton didn't rival the Sears Tower and Hancock Building, there was something exciting about standing on the hotel roof at night, forty stories in the air with no guardrails, surrounded by the gleaming lights of Chicago skyscrapers.

∞∞∞∞

By the time Lonnie graduated from Moody in May and transferred to Northern Illinois University, our relationship was strong and clearly destined for marriage. Thus, for the next two years of college, I was free to focus my attention on the other love in my life: basketball. During Welcome Week, I went down to the gym to play pickup basketball and to size up the talent. I started playing organized basketball in the fourth grade, and playing varsity at a large high school in suburban Chicago had honed my shooting guard skills. Moody had a basketball team that played in the National Christian College Athletic Conference, but given that it was half the size of my high school, I was looking forward to moving from a supporting role in high school to a starring role in college.

During the pickup games, I soon became aware of a short, stocky white guy sporting black horn-rimmed safety glasses kept in place by an elastic band encircling his head (these were known as Kurt Rambis glasses back then). Despite the deceptive appearance, John Avery had the smoothest shooting stroke I had ever witnessed, with his perfect release ending with his right pinkie extended and the ball usually nestling into the net. In addition, there was Drew Anderson, a six foot two redhead from Paw Paw, Michigan, who, strangely enough, seemed to have pogo sticks for legs. Concluding that my best path to playing basketball at Moody was not at shooting guard, I spent the next three years as the starting point guard, capitalizing on the fact that in the Christian college basketball world, one doesn't need foot speed to excel in that position.

As a training ground for zealous Christians intent on full-time ministry, Moody attracted a fair number of older, more mature students, some of whom played basketball. The basketball team, therefore, became the most spiritually formative part of my Moody education. In countless hours on the court, in the team vans, and at Ponderosa Steakhouse after games, I interacted with students who were emotionally and spiritually more mature than me. Gradually they rubbed away my self-centered, materialistic veneer and demonstrated to me a better way of living. For example, there was Jon Lunow, who grew up as a missionary kid in the jungles of Irian Jaya and serves as a missionary in East Asia today; Andy Keller, a six foot eight future missionary pilot who, during the team's Mexico trip, acquired the nickname "El Bow" due to his sharp elbows that inadvertently found their way to both opponents' and teammates' heads; Shawn DeMoss, a former NCAA Division I football player who functioned as the team pastor; Eric Venable, a tall, blond Californian who became a lifelong friend and who pastors a church today in Silicon Valley; and Dave Sheldon, a Minnesotan with an endlessly cheerful demeanor who became the best man in my wedding; and many more. If a Christian college is a "workshop in Christian discipleship," as a professor friend of mine once described it, then the Moody basketball team was my most formative workbench.

While basketball was important to those of us who played, intercollegiate sports did not rank high on the list of Bible college priorities. We played in North Hall, a tiny echo chamber of a gym that included ten rows of bleachers on one side of the court. Thick pads lined the walls that stood three feet behind the baskets. For long-range shooters like John and Drew, stepping across half-court put them nearly within shooting range, although too much arc on a long shot brought the ceiling into play. Unfortunately, North Hall, while a significant home court advantage to us, was too small to be acceptable for national tournament play, which meant that we hosted our first "home" game in the tournament at nearby DePaul University, which we promptly lost.

Our lack of rank at Moody also meant that in order to travel to games throughout the Midwest, we packed ourselves, our coaching staff, two student assistants, and all of our gear into two Dodge eleven-passenger vans. Blake Shaw, a five foot five point guard and talented sleeper from Montana, fit comfortably across the uniform bags in the cargo area and would take his perch there at the beginning of our trips. The van rides became opportunities for deep conversations about faith and life as well as intense, full-contact pillow fights. Years later, when I read about the dangerously top-heavy nature of passenger vans, I marveled that our vehicles never rolled over.

ooooo

The unusual nature of the Moody basketball team highlights the most distinctive feature of Bible colleges like Moody, and one that Virginia Brereton described well in *Training God's Army: The American Bible School, 1880–1940*—an atmosphere marked by intense and sometimes suffocating spirituality.[1] These were, after all, future foot soldiers in God's army—understood in the 1980s in spiritual rather than political terms—so the intensive training began early and pervaded nearly everything. During my first week in the eighteenth floor of Culbertson Hall, a freshman moved his mattress into the storage closet, where it remained for the year. He was preparing to be a missionary in Africa and concluded that sleeping on plywood would be good training. I'm still not sure where he got the idea that Africans don't have soft beds, but the action clearly indicated that I was among spiritual athletes who were playing above my level.

While sleeping on plywood was not the norm, spiritual activities and expectations pervaded Moody culture. Classes invariably opened in prayer, and because most classrooms included an old upright piano and hymnals, it was not uncommon for the professor to summon one of the students to the piano for an opening song (somehow every class seemed to contain at least one student who could sight-read hymn music). Mandatory chapel took place daily at 10:00 a.m. in Torrey-Gray Auditorium. Students signed in on a sheet posted to the wall and sat alphabetically so that attendance could be verified from the balcony above.

Every February, the school celebrated D. L. Moody's birthday by suspending classes for a week and inviting famous preachers from across the country to a weeklong Bible conference, known as Founder's Week, held in nearby Moody Memorial Church. One speaker remarked on his lifelong devotion to reading the Bible, "Cut me and I bleed Scripture" (my internal response was, "Cut me and I bleed *Sports Illustrated*"). My father, a former church music leader and an expert at orchestrating public events, was in charge of the conference. Thus, I served as the van driver who picked up celebrity speakers from their hotel and drove them to Moody Church. Doing so entitled me to personal conversations with many of the heroes of 1980s evangelicalism such as Stuart and Jill Briscoe, Jerry Falwell Sr., Howard Hendricks, Bill Hybels, John MacArthur, Josh McDowell, and Chuck Swindoll. While some of them had their flaws and may have taken a turn for the worse later, in my experience these individuals were invariably sincere, kind, and deeply committed to their work.

One day each spring semester, classes were canceled so that students and faculty could spend the entire day praying individually, in groups, and as an entire community. While I enjoyed the energy and bustle of Founder's Week, I lacked the patience and presence of mind to appreciate the Day of Prayer. Such an attitude tended to describe my approach to daily devotions in general, which were a big part of Bible college culture. The truly spiritual Christian was expected to spend significant time each morning in private prayer and Bible reading; some even claimed to spend an hour a day in devotions. For a time, I achieved a half hour in morning devotions, but invariably my mind wandered or I slept through my alarm clock. The lack of a meaningful "quiet time" generally remained a matter of guilt to me.

The other main annual event was missions conference in the fall semester. For a week, foreign missionaries, many of them Moody alums, invaded the campus and set up information booths outside the dining room. The more prominent missionaries had speaking time in chapel and in special evening services. The week closed with an invitation by Moody president George Sweeting. While the organ played, Dr. Sweeting invited those who had experienced a clear call to full-time Christian service to come to the front of the auditorium for prayer, which drew a large response. Next, an invitation to come forward was issued to those who had not received a definite call but were open to receiving such a call. A final invitation was issued to those who felt called to come forward to pray for those who were called or who were open to being called. By then, few stragglers like myself were left standing in the pews.

It's not that I was a spiritual rebel at Moody; I just found my own spiritual outlook and future plans moving in a different direction from the dominant culture at Moody. In fact, the missions conference expressed what in retrospect seemed to me to be a major weakness of conservative evangelical culture at the time: a constricted understanding of what "serving God" in one's vocation meant, or could mean. One of the achievements of the Protestant Reformers was a revaluing of human work. As John Calvin wrote in the *Institutes of the Christian Religion*, "there is no employment so mean and sordid as not to appear truly respectable, and be deemed highly important in the sight of God."

Bible colleges, however, tended to rank professions on a scale from sacred to secular. For men, the top two ranks were pastors and missionaries. For women, the epitome of ministry was missionary service, in which opportunities for significant work outside the home were often broader overseas than in the United States, or being a pastor's wife. For the rest of us, the main purpose of one's career was basically to earn money to help support the local church and the missionaries who were out there doing God's work. Students like me, who found themselves drawn to careers elsewhere, were left with little means of understanding their future calling in a theological sense.

For all students, however, regardless of future calling, "practical Christian ministry," or PCM, was a weekly requirement. In some ways, Bible colleges were years ahead of the rest of academia in grasping the value of service learning; they just applied the term in more narrowly Christian categories. Thus, every student had a weekly Christian ministry assignment such as after-school Bible clubs, working in a rescue mission, and the like. Sometimes the ministry was tailored to one's major. Lonnie played piano in a nursing home for several semesters, while I, a Bible/theology major, spent a year teaching children's Sunday school at an urban black church.

For at least one semester, each student had a personal evangelism requirement. For me, that consisted of a semester of the dreaded "van visitation" during my first year. One afternoon each week, seven other students and I loaded ourselves into a van (probably the same one that transported the basketball team across the Midwest) and drove to a Chicago neighborhood. Ours happened to be a Polish Catholic neighborhood on the Near West Side. There we would pair up male and female, and our assignment was to knock on doors and share the gospel with local residents. Our strategic entry into the conversation was a "religious questionnaire" that we would request of the resident when he or she answered the door. I was painfully shy, and my partner, Jennifer, was just plain cynical, so our general strategy was to knock softly on the door, wait for three seconds hoping that no one would answer, then scamper off to another house. We also spent ample time wandering up and down a block and evaluating whether certain homes looked like decent prospects or not. The strategy generally enabled us to limit our evangelistic attempts to about four or five per week.

To my annoyance, during the same semester Lonnie hit the PCM jackpot: she and two male students were assigned to a local church that was employing Evangelism Explosion, a tool developed by Florida pastor D. James Kennedy that was quite popular at the time. The church kept a record of visitors to its Sunday service, then Lonnie and her colleagues, armed with the Evangelism Explosion manual, were supposed to visit the visitors on Tuesday evening to ask them fun icebreaker questions such as, "If you were to die today and God were to ask you, 'Why should I let you into heaven?' what would you say?" Fortunately for Lonnie, the church had few visitors, and those who did visit seemed to be away from home on Tuesday evenings, so she and her partners usually ended up at Bakers Square eating pie for much of the evening.

Like all college students, however, Moody kids managed to have plenty of fun; they just had to be more creative about doing so. Televisions were prohibited in dorm rooms—a rule stemming from religious zeal but which actually had tremendous educational value for young adults who thus learned to create their own forms of entertainment. *Late Show with David Letterman* was becoming popular at the time, and while we couldn't watch it in our rooms, we learned that one of David's stunts was dropping objects from a tall building to watch them explode on the street below. Being in the city, Moody grew up as well as out, which meant that Culbertson Hall was nineteen stories high. For a time, therefore, our nights in Culbertson Hall became a continuous experiment in which objects pilfered from the dining room made the most satisfying explosion when dropped from our eighteenth-story windows onto Chicago Avenue. A house sitting a half-block south of Culbertson had a swimming pool in its tiny backyard, so we would attempt to reach the pool with leftover oranges. For months afterward, I pictured the residents stepping outside in the morning and wondering how oranges managed to drop from the sky into their yard overnight.

Of course, as typical young adult males, some students inevitably took things too far. It was widely rumored that one resident of the nineteenth floor had his friends hold him by the ankles and dangle him outside the window so that he could knock on the window of his rather startled neighbors one floor below. Apparently this was the culmination of a series of interesting escapades that led to his expulsion. Other enjoyable study breaks included all-floor fights with jumbo marshmallows—which leave impressive welts on bare skin—and the occasional "water night" when the drains of the large common shower/bathroom would be covered, all of the faucets turned on, and the tile floor be converted into a water slide.

In general, however, aside from some generally harmless diversions, Moody students were earnest, focused, and responsible. Evenings generally consisted of diligent study and conversations in dormitory lounges that were blessedly devoid of TV and the Internet. In fact, aside from the basketball team, the most formative peer influences on me were the "missionary kids" who had grown up overseas, often in remote locations. Many came from boarding schools such as Faith Academy in the Philippines, Rift Valley Academy in Africa, or Black Forest Academy in Germany, and they formed something of an elite subculture at Moody. One group of missionary kids, led by the Lunow twins, Dave and Jon, lived on the fourteenth floor, and I loved to head downstairs at night and listen to their stories of life in the jungles of Irian Jaya—of angels with flaming swords that hostile villagers saw at night protecting their parents; of black mambas dropping out of kitchen cupboards; of their parents translating the Bible into the native language and also performing surgeries and amputations; of six-year-old kids being dropped off at boarding school and squatting on their feet atop the classroom desks because they had never encountered a chair before.

These experiences were worlds away from my middle-class suburban upbringing, and they awakened in me a desire for travel long before I had ever been anywhere beyond the United States. Of course, many of these missionary kids had traumatic life and family experiences. Some wrestled with their faith and ended up leaving the evangelicalism of their parents altogether. Unintentionally, however, missionary kids at Moody also fostered a healthy counterculture critique of American consumerism. Moody students did not go to college to get a degree as a ticket to a lucrative career. They wanted to make a difference in the world, and Bible college was the first step. I didn't need Bible professors to encourage me to look beyond a good salary for significance; I saw it modeled by other students.

ooooo

And what about academics at Moody? In comparison to my subsequent experiences at Michigan and Notre Dame, academics played less of a role for me at Moody than it would later. Moody has made significant progress academically in the past few decades, but in the 1980s, its educational approach was dominated by a theology known as "dispensational premillennialism." To simplify a complex topic, dispensationalists divide biblical history into distinct historical periods, or dispensations. We are currently in the church age and await Christ's physical return to earth in order to institute his reign on earth for a thousand years (hence the "premillennialism").

Dispensational premillennialism went hand in hand with an extremely literalistic view of the Bible as a source of factual information about God and the world. As the nineteenth-century theologian Charles Hodge once asserted, "The Bible is to the theologian what nature is to the man. It is his storehouse of facts."[2] The words of the Bible thus are viewed as "inerrant," that is, free from error, as defined by modern scientific rationality. The doctrine of inerrancy tends to create an "all or nothing" approach to biblical interpretation: if any part of Scripture can be shown to be inaccurate or untrue, then the Bible is no longer an inspired, trustworthy source of God's revelation. Whatever its merits as a school of biblical interpretation, dispensationalism tended to put a damper on creative or critical thinking in the classroom. Bible and theology classes at Moody tended to consist of accumulating as much biblical information as possible in order to regurgitate it on a test; or in the case of theology, learning the biblical passages that support the doctrine of the Fall, the virgin birth, the second coming, and other essential beliefs.

The gateway course for Moody students was Dr. Benware's Old Testament survey class, taught in Alumni Auditorium, which most freshmen took their first semester. Dr. Benware was a gifted lecturer, and his classes were informative and engaging. The overall goal of the course, however, seemed to be data acquisition—to learn as much Old Testament content as possible. The class grade was based largely on four 100-question multiple-choice exams, much feared by students, which drilled down into the names and characteristics of the judges, the various kings of Judah, the dates of the Babylonian captivity, and so on. Being adept at learning information, I prided myself on earning the highest score in the class, though my fellow classmate Bryan O'Neal, now a Moody vice president, remembers things differently.

Two Bible courses best revealed Moody's educational approach in the 1980s—angelology and Daniel/Revelation. Angelology was taught by a Bible professor who had a reputation as an expert in demonic activity and of having performed exorcisms, so students referred to him as the Ghostbuster. The course surveyed all the biblical passages that refer to angelic beings, spirits, and Satan to present a systematic overview of the subject. The notion that angelology could be a science on a par with other "-ologies," such as anthropology and physiology, vividly illustrated the view of Scripture as a "storehouse of facts" that characterized Bible college education at the time.

Daniel/Revelation was based on the belief that the prophetic passages in the Old Testament were to be interpreted literally and found their culmination in certain passages in the book of Revelation. Thus, biblical scholars constructed intricate chronological charts to summarize the historical epochs foretold in the book of Daniel and to match them with possible future fulfillments. Ironically, since prophetic literature was by nature ambiguous, Daniel/Revelation was also a course in which students honed their critical thinking skills by arguing for one particular interpretation against another, and intense debates were waged between pre-, mid-, and posttribulationists and other ideological camps. Four decades later, it's difficult to appreciate just how strong prophecy belief, including an imminent end of the world, was among evangelicals in the 1980s. And while I don't miss such preoccupation with the end times, at least it did tend to encourage a healthy skepticism about modern society and discourage the tendency to equate America with the kingdom of God. I suspect that prophecy belief's decline among modern

American evangelicals may have less to do with any change in biblical interpretation and more to do with a reawakened desire among many to reassert control over American culture and politics.

Generally speaking, therefore, Moody did little to awaken my interest in learning, let alone embark on a career in academics. I attended class, studied enough to get As while tutoring my dormitory friends into getting Bs, and kept a crossword puzzle in my notebook to make it through class when necessary. There were, however, a few professors who planted seeds in my consciousness that bore fruit later. Typically they were eccentric or out of the mainstream, and some of them didn't stay at Moody very long.

For example, there was Miss Beam, a single female English professor, perhaps a bit awkward socially but nevertheless loved by students. We never asked what she thought of Moody's academic culture of dispensationalism, but she clearly loved poetry and literature, whatever the genre, and sought to instill that love in future Christian workers. Once a friend and I were sitting in our usual back-row seats and Miss Beam was reading aloud a poem by Carl Sandburg. The poem was written out in our textbooks as well, and so my eyes scanned down the poem and landed on the word "dogshit." I pointed it out to my friend, and we waited eagerly to see whether Miss Beam would skip over the word (this was Bible school, after all) or pronounce it. When she arrived at the line, she drew in her breath and gave out the heartiest "dogshit" I have ever heard. I don't remember the poem, but I do remember that for Miss Beam, the integrity of the poem trumped the taboos of a Bible college.

Then there was our History of Doctrine professor, a man who seemed to wear a perpetual mischievous grin on his face. I'm not sure how his hiring was approved by the Bible Department, but his underlying purpose in the class was to show students that Christian beliefs did not exist in a pristine time capsule from New Testament times but had changed over time in response to historical and cultural influences. To make sure we got the message, we were all assigned a research project tracing the history of beliefs about the atonement from Paul to the present. I later heard that this professor left Moody before a book he was writing on a controversial topic appeared in print.

Another outlier was our professor for Bible introduction. This course explored how the books of the Bible came to be written, and how the biblical canon emerged over the first few centuries of Christianity. In other words, the course served as a tour of the kitchen in the back of the restaurant, showing the messy manner in which much of Scripture came to be—an approach ripe for undermining a simplistic understanding of the Bible as miraculously descended from on high. The professor was careful in his approach, since the course content was a potential minefield in a place like Moody, but at the end of the semester, he encouraged students to take time over the summer to compile a harmony of the Gospels.

I took up the challenge, and it didn't take long for me to give up arranging the four accounts of the life of Jesus into any kind of coherent chronological order. And what was I do to with the accounts of Jesus sending out his disciples in Matthew 10 and Mark 6? In Matthew, Jesus tells his disciples not to take anything with them, "not even a tunic." In Mark, he tells them to take nothing for the journey "except a tunic." Clearly, Matthew and Mark couldn't both be right; one of them got Jesus's words wrong. The typical response, that the "original manuscripts" were correct and the discrepancy is a later error in translation, wasn't very satisfying either. What good to us is an inerrant document that doesn't exist? Then there were the gospel accounts of the death of Judas. In Matthew, Judas hangs himself; in Luke, he falls off a cliff and his insides spill out. The literalist solution is to assert that both accounts are correct: Judas attempted to hang himself, but the rope broke so he fell down the hill. Such explanations sounded similar to the "epicycles" devised by medieval astronomers as they sought to maintain a geocentric universe amid the challenge of Copernicus.

Of course, none of these questions about the Bible were original to me, nor did they need to be fatal to any mature, nuanced understanding of biblical inspiration and authority. But given the "all or nothing" biblical hermeneutic that I had absorbed, combined with a desire for intellectual integrity, these discoveries were troubling, to say the least, and raised doubts about my inherited evangelical beliefs. I began to perceive myself not just as one of the few Christians left standing in the pews during the missions conference altar call, but possibly not a true believer at all.

Fortunately, there was one other Moody professor who opened the door to a wider intellectual world: John Walton. Unlike most of the Bible faculty who had been trained at Dallas Theological Seminary, Dr. Walton earned his PhD in Old Testament from Hebrew Union College. He combined an orthodox belief in the Bible as God's unique revelation with a fervent commitment to interpreting the Old Testament in its ancient historical and cultural context. In other words, he sought to understand the Bible as it would have been understood by a Hebrew reader of the day, not through the cultural lens of twentieth-century American evangelicalism.

Dr. Walton didn't preach historical-critical biblical interpretation to his students, but when I took his course on Isaiah, the difference from other classes was unmistakable. For other Bible professors, a book such as Isaiah was a complicated puzzle of passages that predicted the future, and the job of the reader was to decode these passages and apply them to future events. Thus the passages describing "Lucifer" were, for evangelicals, references to Satan, who had been the head angel in heaven before rebelling against God and being cast down to hell. In one particularly memorable class session, Dr. Walton carefully explained and showed us that, read in historical context, the Lucifer passages referred to a king of the day—probably Nebuchadnezzar—not to some sort of demonic being. A student in the class raised his hand and asked, "So, what am I supposed to do with my angelology notes?" To which Walton chuckled and replied, "Well, I guess I'm sorry about that."

At the end of the semester, we were required to write a research paper on a particular passage from Isaiah and attempt to interpret it from an ancient Jewish perspective. I chose Isaiah chapter 7, a well-known passage in which the author announces, "Behold, the virgin will conceive and give birth to a son, and call his name Immanuel." Anyone who has heard Handel's *Messiah* knows this passage well as a prophecy about the birth of Christ. As I researched the passage and read commentaries, however, I concluded that the speaker in Isaiah seemed to be referring to a young woman who was actually standing there in King Ahaz's palace, not to Mary and Jesus. So why did Matthew's Gospel apply this passage to the birth of Jesus? I checked other Old Testament passages that are quoted in the Gospels, and I came to the conclusion that the gospel writers had a habit of creatively borrowing Old Testament passages—and seemingly misappropriating some passages, from our perspective—for their own purposes. When it came time to turn in my term paper, I was nervous: my conclusion didn't seem to fit with how Christians are supposed to read Old Testament prophecy. To my pleasant surprise, however, my paper received an A. Moreover, Dr. Walton sent me a handwritten note telling me that I showed potential as a scholar and encouraging me to consider a career in academics.

In retrospect, Dr. Walton's significance wasn't that he convinced me to become a biblical scholar—clearly I didn't become one. Rather, I encountered a Christian intellectual who diligently sought to understand the data on its own terms rather than resting in inherited assumptions or easy platitudes. The same dedication to the subject for its own sake that led Miss Beam to exclaim "dogshit" in English class at a Bible college also prompted Dr. Walton to seek to understand who "Lucifer" was to ancient Hebrews rather than simply categorize him as the devil for modern Christians. In other words, Dr. Walton's class was my first entry into a new perspective—that to be a Christian scholar is an act of humility in which we submit ourselves to the data and pay close attention to what God's creation is telling us. It's one way that we as Christians worship God—by loving his creation enough to truly pay attention to it. I only grasped this vaguely at the time, but it would be reinforced at Michigan and Notre Dame by both Christian and non-Christian scholars.

∞∞∞

The longer I work in higher education, the more I'm convinced that a Christian college is basically a contractor. We exist to hire professors who excel at loving God with their minds and loving students, recruit students to put in contact with them, and then get out of the way. Despite its shortcomings, Moody ultimately provided me with a quality education for two primary reasons. First, an alternative, countercultural, residential community existed for me to come into meaningful contact with other students who were either more mature than me or whose experiences differed from mine in significant ways. The basketball team and the missionary kids comprised some of my most formative experiences. Second, I found some professors who, within the narrow confines of a Bible college, asked good questions, modeled humble curiosity, and prodded me in the direction of a deeper, more nuanced Christian faith. In retrospect, Moody provided a fertile seedbed that would come alive with a healthy infusion of skepticism and critical thinking from one of the nation's premier public universities.

CORPORATE INTERLUDE

On May 23, 1987, I graduated from Moody Bible Institute and packed up my dormitory room. The next day, Lonnie and I drove to her family's farmhouse in Mount Joy, Pennsylvania, and were married the following Saturday. In his book *The Curmudgeon's Guide to Getting Ahead*, sociologist Charles Murray describes two types of marriages—mergers and start-ups. In a merger marriage, two successful midcareer professionals combine their operations into a joint venture. In a start-up, two young adults fall in love, get married, and figure out life together. Lonnie and I were definitely the latter. Fortunately for us, while our families weren't perfect, we both benefited from growing up in stable, two-parent families in which love and loyalty were modeled on a regular basis. We (and especially I, who was a few months removed from tossing oranges from dormitory windows) had much to learn about relationships, communication, personality types, and the like, but we had healthy relational reservoirs to draw from and an instinctive commitment to love each other and work through conflicts no matter how difficult.

The third day of our honeymoon in Vermont provided us with an early lesson on what it meant to marry another human being. We decided to go for a hike in the beautiful Green Mountains. Concluding that a walk on the nearby Appalachian Trail wasn't challenging enough, I drove us to Stratton Mountain, a local ski resort that was closed for the summer. We parked in the empty lot, and I figured that by scrambling up a route directly beneath the chair lift, we could eventually reach the summit (which, of course, is the whole point of hiking). Between the 90 degree temperatures and the swarms of biting black flies that descend on New England in June, the hiking experience quickly went downhill. Lonnie concluded, therefore, that we should turn back and not climb to the summit, which made absolutely no sense to me. She eventually prevailed, and the silent car ride back to our chalet was my first lesson in contrasting personality types—one that I have slowly been learning ever since.

Lonnie had just finished her bachelor's degree in music at Northern Illinois University (NIU) in DeKalb, Illinois. The first agenda item in our start-up marriage, therefore, was for Lonnie to continue on at NIU, earning a master's degree in piano performance, so we moved into a third-floor apartment in DeKalb. Lonnie's wedding gift from her mom, the family's Kawai console piano, began its destiny of being one of the most well-traveled pianos in history.

My role while Lonnie finished graduate school was to provide the income, but what does one with a three-year Bible diploma do for a living? Fortunately, a family friend, Al Cormier, was an executive for TelWatch, a technology start-up company that made software that enabled companies to track and allocate internal charges for phone calls (or something like that). Al secured a position for me at TelWatch as a systems engineer, which was ironic because I had typed my term papers on a Brother typewriter and had never used a computer before. At a lunch meeting early in my time there, a fellow TelWatch employee sketched out for me on a napkin the components of a computer such as a hard drive, floppy drive, and "random access memory." Fortunately I was a quick learner, and after a few weeks of training, I figured out enough of the business to perform my basic job, which was handling first-stage customer support for clients such as hospitals and universities.

Years later as a PhD student, I had a conversation with a fellow student whose advisor had told him, "If you can see yourself doing anything else in life other than becoming an academic, you should do it." The main lesson from my nine months at TelWatch was that I was not wired for the corporate world of nine-to-five office work. Despite its rigors, academia was where I belonged. Every day I would drive a mostly empty stretch of the Illinois Tollway across thirty miles of cornfields between DeKalb and TelWatch's Naperville office and back again, reading the *Lord of the Rings* trilogy by holding a paperback on the top of my steering wheel while I drove. On most days, I would plug away on my computer and phone and occasionally accompany our regional salesperson on client visits, after which he would stop at a restaurant for a meal and two martinis. Since TelWatch was a start-up company, I saw new employees added to the ranks when business was good, then saw them let go when sales lagged. I managed to keep my job during the down times most likely due to Al's influence, but it probably made life easier for him and the organization when I eventually left to resume college studies.

In retrospect, it seems that I had developed something of an immature academician's disdain for the daily grind of corporate life and for jobs that mainly consisted of routine and habitual tasks. Later I came to better appreciate the discipline and commitment of those who get up in the morning and do their job day in and day out, not only to support a family but to accomplish some good in the world. At the time, however, life behind a desk seemed soul killing from the perspective of my budding intellectual idealism. Moreover, I had no theological categories to understand the work that most adults do as anything more than a necessary way to earn a paycheck in a capitalist society. Such categories would come later. When I moved into academic administration, I learned that the daily lives of deans and provosts aren't much different from those of clerks and managers, and that a regular routine is a good way for organizations to enable their employees to work together while also preserving spaces in life for other things.

Amid a year of figuring out marriage and working at TelWatch, two seemingly unrelated experiences stand out. First, in late January, Lonnie and I accompanied our local church's youth group to a Chicago Bulls basketball game during a record cold snap. We arrived back at our church in Sugar Grove, Illinois, after midnight and began driving back to DeKalb on an empty country road with the temperature at 25 degrees below zero. Halfway home, the "antifreeze" in our old Honda Accord froze and the engine overheated and blew a head gasket. With no blankets in the car, we faced the choice of walking to a light far off in the distance to ask for help or huddling in the car until a vehicle came along in the morning. Amazingly, ten minutes later a man drove by in a pickup who was on his way to DeKalb, and he drove us home.

A couple of months later, during a visit to TelWatch's headquarters in Boulder, Colorado, I was hiking in the surrounding foothills with my brother-in-law, Ken, who lived in Denver. This was a former silver mining region, and amid our boulder scrambling, we came across some old mining caves. Wandering into the pitch black of one of them, Ken decided to stop and use his camera flash to see what was ahead of us. The instant flash of light revealed a yawning abyss three feet in front of us. We threw a rock in the hole to see how deep it was, and the rock echoed down hundreds of feet of mining shaft. Sufficiently sobered, we continued to climb around the rocks but avoided caves after that.

I bring up these two unrelated and rather unspectacular experiences because, viewed in retrospect and combined with subsequent life events, they served as lessons to me about how tenuous our lives actually are. A few years later, as a graduate student at Notre Dame, I read Jonathan Edwards's sermon "Sinners in the Hands of an Angry God" for an American religion class taught by the Reverend Jonathan Himes. Himes, a cheerful Catholic priest, had little affinity for Edwards's stark Puritan view of human depravity and predestination. Rather, his interest in assigning Edwards's sermon was to impress upon students the "iffy-ness of human existence," as Himes described it. Like a sinner ignorantly walking across a floor with rotten boards, we think we are in control of our lives when in fact so much of life is precarious and depends on God's constant provision and protection. Many times over the past decades, I've wondered how often and in what ways God imperceptibly protects us from disaster, or just gently leads us away from trouble, and how different life for Lonnie and others would have been if Ken and I had taken two more steps into that Colorado cave.

At any rate, by the spring of 1988, when Lonnie finished her master's degree, I was ready to put the corporate world behind me and resume my academic journey at the University of Michigan. Why Michigan? As with Moody, it seemed a natural step to take. My parents were both from rural southeast Michigan, and some of my earliest memories consisted of cheering for the Wolverines on our black and white television against that school in Ohio. Moreover, my older sister Kim, after finishing her time at Moody, completed her degree at Michigan. During our first year of marriage, Lonnie and I visited Kim, who was living in an international house with students from several different countries, and I fell in love with Ann Arbor's academic and cosmopolitan culture. What sealed the deal was that Michigan was willing to accept most of my Moody Bible Institute courses as transfer credits, which meant that with two years of full-time work, I could complete a bachelor's degree at Michigan. In August 1988, therefore, Lonnie and I moved to Ann Arbor to embark on a very different type of college experience from my first.

ooooo

TWO

Academic Awakening

W ITH SOME HELP from friends, Lonnie and I muscled the Kawai and our other possessions up two flights of stairs to a tiny third-floor apartment in Observatory Lodge, an old Tudor-style building with a manually operated elevator that sat just down the street from the University of Michigan observatory. The building served as housing for married students without children, and getting into the building spared us from being relegated to the nether region known as North Campus, where most married students lived.

Among the public research universities of the world, the University of Michigan ranks as one of the best. Of course, that's what a devoted university alum would be expected to say, especially at a school whose fight song proclaims, "the leaders and best," but the numbers support that claim. Established in 1817, Michigan is one of the oldest public universities in the United States. It consistently ranks among the top American universities in the *U.S. News and World Report* rankings, and is the only US public university to be included in the top twenty-five in the Q5 World University Rankings. Other elite universities have students and faculty of Michigan's caliber, but few of them do quality academics at such scale. The average Michigan ACT score range is 31–34, meaning that there are about forty-four thousand student brainiacs roaming the streets and bars of Ann Arbor. When you add over six thousand professors who are significant scholars in their fields, you get an extraordinary amount of intellectual horsepower packed into a few square miles of Upper Midwest terrain.

Religiously and culturally, Michigan feels different from other Midwest universities. The university figures prominently in George Marsden's seminal work, *The Soul of the American University: From Protestant Establishment to Established Nonbelief,* which chronicles the gradual secularization of American higher education over the past two centuries. Like most American universities in the 1800s, Michigan was founded by Protestants and was in many ways a thoroughly Christian institution. All of the university's professors affirmed the Christian faith, and President Henry Tappan delivered an annual lecture series entitled "Evidences of the Christian Religion." Students attended chapel daily and church twice on Sunday.[3]

Over the course of the twentieth century, Michigan not only moved away from Christianity but acquired a reputation as one of America's most secular and socially progressive universities. Students for a Democratic Society, one of the principal organizations of the New Left of the 1960s, was the brainchild of University of Michigan student Tom Hayden and held its first convention at the university in 1960. Moreover, Ann Arbor's prominent place in the hippie movement stemmed from the city's famously lax policies for possession and use of marijuana. The annual Hash Bash is a longtime spring tradition on campus, although its distinctive status has waned with the legalization of cannabis in Michigan and many other states.

Another of the university's distinctives is that it tends to have a higher Jewish demographic than other Midwest universities. Michigan has a reputation as the backup option for Jewish students in the Northeast who do not get into Harvard, Princeton, or Yale, which means that the university receives a steady stream of high-achieving students from places such as New York City and Boston. In 2021, Jewish students made up 16 percent of the university's undergraduate population, and the Jewish campus support organization Hillel listed Michigan number five among the top sixty Jewish universities in the United States. Ann Arbor is home to Zingerman's, the best-known Jewish delicatessen west of New York

City, and the town itself has a decidedly East Coast feel compared to other Midwest college towns.

ooooo

In light of Michigan's high-powered academics, its counterculture roots, and its cosmopolitanism, it's no surprise that conservative Christians would view the university as not necessarily friendly to Christian faith. I had been warned in advance about Michigan's pervasive secularism, and to some extent such warnings did have merit. Coming from a Bible college, I was probably better able than most to see how Michigan's commitment to secularism functioned as a kind of religious dogmatism in its own right. When I arrived in the fall of 1988, Michigan had just approved a campus speech code that prohibited "negative speech" toward specific groups, and which was the first of its kind to be struck down by a US district court. The attempt to identify and prohibit cultural taboos did seem ironically similar to some of my experiences at Moody.

Early in my time there, I attended an evening lecture in which a student asked the faculty presenter something to the effect of "but what are we supposed to do about evangelical Christians?" The professor responded, "Well, I don't particular like them myself," before going on to affirm the importance of not excluding any particular group from university life. I furtively checked to see if I was emoting any subtle indicator of my evangelical identity. There were some Christian groups on campus that thrived on the sense of antagonism between Michigan and traditional Christianity. During my first year at Michigan, Campus Crusade (now called Cru) invited the popular evangelist and apologist Josh McDowell, author of *Evidence That Demands a Verdict*, to lead a widely publicized event on campus, which sparked some vigorous discussions between Christians and non-Christians on the Diag and other campus locations. My own personality, however, did not resonate with Campus Crusade's aggressive approach to campus evangelism, which brought back harrowing memories of van visitation at Moody.

Aside from a few isolated experiences and the sometimes comically extreme liberalism of student editorials in the *Michigan Daily*,

27

however, I encountered little anti-Christian hostility at Michigan. In fact, two of my professors were known as evangelicals, one of whom was Martin Gaskell, an astronomy professor who attended the same church as Lonnie and me. In his concluding lecture. Dr. Gaskell gave an argument for a Creator based on the finely tuned complexity of the universe, for which the students gave him a rousing ovation.

What I did discover at Michigan was that for all of their short-comings, modern universities still produce some of the best that human culture has to offer. Long before I had a theological category of "common grace" for the concept, I learned that non-Christians can excel at "culture making," as Andy Crouch calls it, that expresses the goodness of creation. Much of this lesson was in music. Observatory Lodge is a short walk from Hill Auditorium, one of the most acoustically-rich performance halls in the world. Through discounted student tickets, Lonnie and I were able to experience the musical genius of Kathleen Battle, Leonard Bernstein, Benny Goodman, and Yo-Yo Ma.

And then of course there was sports. Like a medieval town with a cathedral at the highest point, Michigan's main campus sits below Michigan Stadium—the Big House—where the communal religious event known as college football occurs on autumn Saturday afternoons with over 100,000 observants, and where that profound collective ritual, the Wave, achieved perfection in the stadium's perfectly enclosed structure. On game days, Lonnie and I would join thousands of other Michigan students on the long pilgrimage up to the Big House in the morning and return in the late-afternoon dusk, usually with a stop at Cottage Inn Pizza along the way. While Michigan is known as a football school, strangely enough, the men's basketball team won the NCAA national championship during our first year there. The postgame celebration on State Street provided me with my first opportunity to see a car turned on its side by celebrating students.

Above all, however, Michigan awakened in me a vision for the life of the mind, and how the vigorous pursuit of truth is fostered by a university community and in turn adds vitality to that community. It is sometimes assumed that professors at top-tier research universities focus on their scholarship while graduate students teach the undergraduates, but that was by no means my experience at Michigan. The tenured professors at Michigan who wrote the books that were used by other universities also taught us undergraduates, and if they didn't enjoy it, they certainly faked it well.

I arrived at Michigan with a case of "imposter syndrome," wondering whether a Moody Bible Institute graduate could really cut it at a place like Michigan. That question was answered for me in the middle of the fall semester in a class session in Dr. Beauchamp's History of American Literature course. We were assigned to read "Bartleby, the Scrivener," a mid-nineteenth-century short story by Herman Melville. Beauchamp began the class discussion with the question, "How would you describe the author's tone in this story?" Some of the usual first-responder students raised their hands and answered, but their replies didn't seem to satisfy the professor. It seemed to me that the story was something of a satire, and that the students were overthinking the text and failing to see Melville's attempt at humor (which, understandably, does not always carry well across the centuries). Sheepishly I raised my hand for the first time in the semester, and when Dr. Beauchamp looked my way, I remarked, "It's humor; the story is supposed to be funny." Beauchamp's smiling nod of satisfaction boosted my confidence in my academic abilities, and still serves as a reminder, thirty years later, of the tremendous and often unknown impact that teachers' actions in the classroom can have on students.

I chose history as my major for two reasons. First, it consists primarily of stories and so is interesting; second, since there is a history of every subject, it allowed me to study pretty much whatever I wanted to. At Michigan I took courses in the history of Rome, the American Revolution, American intellectual history, the early Middle Ages, as well as an assortment of courses in English, philosophy, social sciences, and two years of German. Somehow, through the generous acceptance of transfer credits from Moody, my astronomy course with Dr. Gaskell was the only natural science course that I ever took in college, and I escaped mathematics altogether.

I learned several academic virtues through my classes at Michigan. For example, the first week of George Mavrodes's Philosophy of Religion course taught me a lesson in taking responsibility for one's learning. Monday and Wednesday classes consisted of lectures on particular topics in our readings, and Friday's class was an open discussion of themes from the week. On the first Friday of the semester, Dr. Mavrodes, a soft-spoken, gray-haired man with piercing blue eyes, walked into the classroom, stood at the front, and asked us what questions we had from the week's readings. What followed was about fifteen seconds of awkward silence, after which Dr. Mavrodes said, "Well, okay, have a good weekend," and walked out of the room. I don't know if this was an intentional strategy by Dr. Mavrodes or just his instinctive response, but the lesson was clear: students are responsible for the learning in this course, and we need to come to class on Friday prepared for discussion—which we invariably did for the rest of the semester.

Another course, Diane Hughes's History of the Early Middle Ages, taught me the intellectual virtue of empathy (though as we will see later, I still had a ways to go on that one). In the course of the semester, and in reading some of her works, it became clear that Dr. Hughes was far from a Christian herself. Nevertheless, as a historian of an era deeply shaped by Christianity, she demonstrated an understanding of and appreciation for the church fathers, Pope Gregory, and other features of early Christianity that rivals that of any Christian historian. While she did not share their worldview, as a student I can't recall ever hearing any tone of mockery or condescension in her portrayal of early Christianity.

Furthermore, long before I encountered George Marsden's argument in *The Outrageous Idea of Christian Scholarship* that all scholars bring certain assumptions and paradigms to their subjects, I saw this demonstrated in Kenneth Lockridge's American Revolution course. Undergraduate history courses usually consist of a detailed chronological walk through the subject, with exams covering a dense array of names, dates, and events. Lockridge, however, took a different approach. We spent the first few weeks of the course surveying the historical nuts and bolts of the Revolutionary era, and then took an exam. For the rest of the semester, we explored and discussed various historical interpretations of and debates surrounding the Revolution. To what extent was the Revolution generated by the economic interests of wealthy merchants? How important was religion to the Revolution? How socially radical was the Revolution, and to what extent did it disrupt the social hierarchies of the day? I didn't always appreciate the complexity of Lockridge's approach at the time, but later I came to realize that he was trying to get undergraduates to think like real historians. Years later, when I wrote a book, *Why College Matters to God*, that attempted to show the importance of different worldviews on education, examples from Lockridge's class found their way into the introductory chapter.

In *The Art of Teaching*, writer and critic Jay Parini explains the importance of teachers creating a "persona" in the classroom—an authentic but somewhat exaggerated extension of their real selves—and I saw that exemplified by two professors in particular. The Renaissance was a sophomore-level course consisting of sixty students sitting in rows of old wooden desk-chairs in a large, rectangular classroom with a tile floor, drab beige walls, and a large chalkboard at the front. Each class session, Professor Marvin Becker, an elderly gentleman with disheveled hair, a rumpled tweed jacket, and khaki pants, would slowly walk into class carrying a tattered oversized leather book bag. He would proceed to scribble on the board a few phrases such as "Dante's *Inferno*," "Realism," or "*Studia Humanitatis*." These served as his lecture notes and PowerPoint slides, and he would then sit down and speak for seventy-five minutes on the topics at hand, occasionally fielding questions or reading from primary texts. What he lacked in cutting-edge, "guide on the side" pedagogy, he made up for in natural eloquence and sheer brilliance. As I discovered later, he was also probably the world's foremost scholar on the subject at the time.

Another memorable persona was Russell Fraser, an English professor who taught a popular Shakespeare course. Although it was a discussion-centered literature course, the class was held in a small auditorium to accommodate the hundred-plus students who enrolled in the course. Most class periods consisted of a discussion of a Shakespearean play, and I lost track of how many we read over the course of the semester. Dr. Fraser never gave quizzes to verify whether students had done the reading; his direct engagement with them regarding the material conveyed the message: "Of course you read the text. This is college; why would you not read the text?" Dr. Fraser didn't lecture—or at least never seemed to—but instead walked the aisles of the auditorium engaging with individual students about themes or questions in the play in what seemed to me at the time to be a natural, improvised conversation that nevertheless somehow resulted in a conclusion. After years as a teacher myself, I came to realize just how difficult and well honed Dr. Fraser's method was, and that the seeming effortlessness of his class discussions resulted from years of practice and skilled preparation. As it was once said about Fred Astaire's dancing, it looked so effortless because he practiced endlessly.

In David Hollinger's American Intellectual History class I learned the power of ideas and the thrill of encountering them through a gifted lecturer. I still vividly recall his lecture on the evolution of Mark Twain's thought toward nihilism, and the intense class discussion of pragmatism as expressed through the writings of William James and John Dewey. Dr. Hollinger was another professor who, like Dr. Gaskell, received an ovation from students as he departed the lecture hall after the last class. Though I never developed the knack for giving engaging lectures myself, I experienced enough of them at Michigan to read any academic article on the death of "sage on the stage" lecturing with a grain of salt.

ooooo

In all, my University of Michigan experience awakened in me a love for ideas, taught me the value of critical thinking, and instilled in me confidence that I brought something to the academic table. While it's an oversimplification, I've often remarked that at Moody I learned to give answers and at Michigan I learned to ask questions. My Michigan education wasn't perfect, however. While Lonnie and I were somewhat involved in a church community in Ann Arbor, Huron Hills Baptist Church, my academic life was largely separate from my Christian faith. On my own, I was reading classic Christian thinkers such as Jonathan Edwards, G. K. Chesterton, and C. S. Lewis, but I had little guidance on how to connect my Christian faith with the stimulating and provocative ideas that I was encountering at Michigan.

This lack of integration between faith and academics was most apparent in my human evolution course, taught by a paleoanthropologist named Milford Wolpoff. Coming from Moody, where I learned in my class on Genesis that God directly created Adam and Eve about six thousand years ago, I was both intrigued by the human evolution course and nervous about it. Dr. Wolpoff, like so many of my Michigan professors, was both a renowned scholar and a charismatic teacher who could hold the attention of a hundred students as he walked the elevated stage of our classroom lecturing on *Australopithecus* and the like. With bushy hair and eyebrows and an ambling gait, he slightly resembled a Neanderthal himself, as he enjoyed pointing out. Concerning religion, Dr. Wolpoff was not antagonistic but simply dismissive. On the first day of class, Dr. Wolpoff exclaimed, "You can believe that God is behind evolution, and that's fine. I may also believe that a little green man is sitting on my shoulder, and every time I turn around, he disappears. There's no way to disprove that scientifically." He then spent the semester providing an account of how *Homo sapiens* evolved over eons through materialistic processes.

I didn't recognize it as such at the time, but Dr. Wolpoff was expressing what evolutionary biologist Stephen Jay Gould called "NOMA," or "non-overlapping magisteria"—that is, that science and religion represent completely different areas of inquiry. Science deals with facts, religion with values, and each should stay in its proper sphere. NOMA didn't help me know what to do with the creation account in Genesis, which seemed to be not just expressing values but making some claims about physical reality as well. But Dr. Wolpoff was an engaging and persuasive teacher, so while I couldn't explain how evolution fit with Genesis, I could bracket those questions for the time being and hold to a designer God who superintended the process, even if science had no way of detecting it. Later I found help in books by Christian scholars such as Francis Collins and, ironically, my former Moody professor John Walton.

In other words, I had no academic mentors, Christian or otherwise, at Michigan. I missed the opportunity to actually get to know and be influenced by my professors, some of whom, such as Dr. Mavrodes, were known to be evangelical Christians. While universities such as Michigan have gotten better at going small in recent years, during my time there, everything from football to classes seemed to exist on a large scale, even my upper-level courses. Other than a senior research seminar entitled "Japan in World War II" that enrolled sixteen students, every course I took at Michigan was large enough to allow introverts like me to fly under the radar and separate education from relationship.

ooooo

By the spring of 1990 I was concluding my time at Michigan and wondering what to do next. One of the last classes I took, Leslie Tentler's course on American religious history, turned out to be the most significant. Toward the end of the semester, we read an orange paperback entitled *Fundamentalism and American Culture: The Shaping of Twentieth Century Evangelicalism*, written a decade earlier by a Calvin College professor named George Marsden. The book was a meticulously researched but readable history of the development of Protestant fundamentalism from the mid-1800s to the early 1900s, culminating in the Scopes monkey trial of 1925. For scholars and observers of American culture, Marsden's text helped them make sense of the rise of the Religious Right in the late 1970s. A certain strand of American Protestants, Marsden showed, had always viewed America as a Christian nation and sought to exercise a "custodial" role over American culture. They became an overlooked subculture after the Scopes trial but emerged again in the 1980s.[4]

To me, however, Marsden's book was more than a way to understand the Religious Right: it was like reading my family history, with historical accounts of D. L. Moody, the formation of Moody Bible Institute, the origins of anti-evolutionism, the belief in biblical inerrancy, even the growth of dispensational premillennialism that had pervaded my Bible courses at Moody. It's difficult to overstate the impact of this book on my own understanding of my Christian faith, and of the value of studying history as a way to understand my beliefs and my community better. It was as if Marsden had ushered me from the restaurant, where the meals were served, back into the kitchen and showed me where the ingredients had come from and how they had been cooked. The experience was both enlightening and disturbing, since some of the ingredients upon further examination seemed to be questionable, and some of the cooking methods less than hygienic. In the hands of a talented scholar such as Marsden, religious history seemed to demonstrate that every faith community, including my own, was composed of some elements that were authentically biblical and others that were quirks of a particular place and time in history. The trick was distinguishing the timeless from the time-bound.

Unbeknownst to me at the time, George Marsden was a leading figure in a larger movement of Christian scholars, especially historians and philosophers, who were attempting to overcome what one of them, Mark Noll, would later call the "intellectual disaster of fundamentalism." The most prominent among them were four professors who had taught together at Calvin College in Grand Rapids, Michigan—George Marsden, Richard Mouw, Alvin Plantinga, and Nicholas Wolterstorff. By the 1980s, Christians in several academic disciplines had created scholarly societies such as the Conference on Faith and History and the Society of Christian Philosophers. In addition, the Institute for the Study of American Evangelicals had been established at Wheaton College to fund scholarly research on evangelicalism.

As a Christian student at Moody and Michigan during the 1980s, I was remarkably unaware of the development of this Christian scholarly community. Until then, my only encounter with Calvin College had been attending an academic conference on Calvin's campus and being surprised to see students and professors smoking cigarettes outside of the buildings between sessions. Soon, however, I was to learn that I was not alone in being impacted by Marsden and his colleagues. For many other young evangelicals and me at the time, Marsden's "orange book" set us on a journey toward becoming Christian scholars ourselves, both to make sense of our own religious experience and to help other Christians better understand—and untangle—the complex knots of religion and culture.

The next logical step for me, therefore, was graduate school. I applied to Michigan and was declined, either because, like most top graduate schools, Michigan prefers to take in students from other undergraduate programs, or because of my unspectacular Graduate Record Exam score, or both. My only other application was to the University of Notre Dame, where one of Marsden's evangelical historian colleagues, Nathan Hatch, served as director of graduate studies. A few weeks later, I received a call from the chair of the History Department offering a full tuition scholarship and a graduate student stipend of $9,000 per year. That seemed to be a pretty clear indicator of the next step, and so in the summer of 1990, Lonnie and I loaded our possessions into a U-Haul and headed to South Bend, Indiana. My academic and spiritual journey was far from over.

oooooo

EUROPEAN INTERLUDE

An important event happened in the middle of my two years at Michigan that I will shoehorn into this gap in the academic narrative. Lonnie and I may have had our differences regarding the best way to hike New England, but we shared a fascination with Europe and a desire to visit there someday. We scrimped and saved during our first two years of marriage, and in late May of 1989, we boarded an overnight flight to Zurich for a three-week tour of Europe by train. I have flown to Europe many times since then, but I never tire of that feeling of waking up from a brief night's sleep, made shorter by the time change, to the smell of airplane coffee and looking out the window to see the sun rising over northern Europe. There's something magical about getting on a plane and landing in a different world, and for me that thrill doesn't diminish with time.

We landed in Zurich on a Sunday morning and took a train to Bern for our first day. The half-timbered houses, centuries-old fountains in town squares, and cobblestone streets were everything that we had anticipated Europe would be. Our next few days were spent visiting the Swiss cities of Geneva and Basel before heading north to Freiburg in southern Germany and traveling by train across the Black Forest. As rookie travelers, we were new not only to Europe but to German wine. Our overnight visit in the charming village of Gunzburg included dinner with a generous serving of German *Weisswein* that resulted in my assisting a wobbly Lonnie back to our hotel for an early bedtime. From there we followed the train route into Salzburg and across northern Austria.

The trip was made possible in part because Lonnie leveraged our Moody Bible Institute missionary connections to secure as much free lodging in Europe as possible. Sometimes the Moody connections produced free housing but other complications as well. Our missionary hosts in Paris were kind and hospitable but were not the ideal introduction to Parisian culture. The husband had written a doctoral dissertation proving that the wine in the Bible was actually unfermented grape juice, and during a brief driving tour of the city, we sped by an interesting-looking building and were informed, "That's the Louvre; there's some great art in there."

Other missionary visits produced better results. Lonnie's parents were friends with a missionary family in Vienna. The father, John, was working as a missionary supporting underground churches in Communist-controlled Eastern Europe. We accompanied him on a visit behind the Iron Curtain into Hungary and Romania, and while Hungary was open to the West, Romania still lay under dictator Nicolae Ceaușescu's iron grip. Because John was known by the Communist authorities and subjected to routine searches, he stashed Bibles and other Christian materials in the bottom of our suitcases, which were unlikely to be searched, and we occupied separate train cars on our journey into Bucharest. Stories of Christian "smugglers" in Communist Europe were legendary during our time at Moody, and it was exciting and nerve-racking to play that role ourselves. The method worked, and while our bags were not searched, as naive tourists we were subjected to an "entry fee" that we later learned from John was simply an extortion by the border guard.

Visitors were required to stay in government-approved hotels, but with John's assistance we dressed up in peasant garb and spent a few nights with a Christian family in their small apartment tucked into one of thousands of drab high-rise apartment buildings. For three days we accompanied John in his meetings with small groups of Christians and toured the sights of Bucharest, often with Ceaușescu's imposing palace, which was under construction, looming in the distance. The darkness and gloom of the city were not only spiritual but literal, due to rotating power outages. It seemed unbelievable that only six months later, Communist regimes would be overthrown across Eastern Europe and Ceaușescu himself would be executed by a firing squad, his palace still incomplete.

Another fortunate by-product of our visit to Romania was meeting another missionary couple working there who were based in Oxford, England—the final destination of our Europe tour. Thus, after returning with John to Vienna, we resorted to more conventional tourist activities and meandered by train from Austria to England. On the way, we experienced unforgettable memories of wandering the canals of Venice, strolling the pebble beaches of Nice, touring Versailles, and crossing the English Channel by hovercraft. After two days amid the spires of Oxford, we boarded a return flight from London's Heathrow Airport to the United States.

While my brief corporate interlude convinced me that I didn't belong in business, this whirlwind tour of eight European countries in three weeks had the opposite effect. It awakened a love for international travel and foreign cultures that would significantly impact my teaching and scholarly career. Lonnie and I would return to Europe for a much longer stay, but that would be two academic degrees, several years of teaching, and four kids later.

ooooo

THREE

A Community of Scholars

O N A WARM SATURDAY evening in September 1990, I found myself, a new graduate student, standing in the University of Notre Dame student section, watching my beloved Wolverines playing football against the Fighting Irish in the season's opening game. Both teams were stacked with future NFL players and ranked in the top five. Michigan started slowly and trailed at halftime, but in the second half they gained the momentum. Leading by a field goal in the fourth quarter, they drove toward our north end zone for the clinching touchdown, only to have quarterback Elvis Grbac throw an interception in the end zone, after which the Irish rallied for a game-winning touchdown. The image is as painfully vivid today as it was thirty years ago; unfortunately, I even remember the intercepting linebacker's name, Michael Stonebreaker. So began my six years at Notre Dame, an institution located somewhere between Moody Bible Institute and the University of Michigan on the higher-education ideological spectrum.

ooooo

The University of Notre Dame du Lac, or Notre Dame, as it is better known, is one of America's oldest and most prominent Catholic universities, and its fight song ranks a close second behind Michigan's (in my opinion). The school was founded in 1842 along the shores of a small lake in northern Indiana. With the influx of

Catholic immigrants, Notre Dame's enrollment and campus grew steadily over the next century, and the school added new colleges and a law school. Its increasing stature, of course, was boosted by the football team, which achieved prominence in the early 1900s under coach Knute Rockne. During Father Theodore Hesburgh's thirty-five-year presidency from 1952 to 1987, Notre Dame developed into the country's preeminent Catholic research university. Today it enrolls more than twelve thousand students and boasts over a thousand professors. Compared to Michigan's sprawling, somewhat chaotic campus, Notre Dame's carefully planned quad and uniform tan-brick architectural style communicate orderliness and calm. The sense of peacefulness is reinforced by the absence of a bustling urban center nearby, other than a few pubs and restaurants just south of campus. In my first visit to Notre Dame in spring of 1990, I expected the university's adjacent city, South Bend, to resemble Ann Arbor, only to discover a somewhat tired Indiana Rust Belt town instead.

Like Michigan, Notre Dame consistently ranks among the top national universities in the *U.S. News and World Report* rankings. Its prestige, however, stems largely from its undergraduate program, not its graduate programs, which are solid but overall not as selective as the Ivies and premier state universities. This fact worked in my favor, since I was able to enroll at Michigan as an undergraduate and Notre Dame as a graduate student, and include both institutions on my résumé. Also, while Notre Dame certainly takes its Catholic identity seriously—every dormitory building, for example, has a priest in residence—its graduate programs tend to wear their Catholicism more lightly. I had great experiences with Catholic professors such as Jay Dolan and Wilson Miscamble, and I enjoyed my first glass of port wine in a class session in Father Himes's dormitory apartment. In general, however, the History Department's ideological approach did not feel distinctively religious. It was certainly a far cry from the conservative religious ethos that dominated nearly all aspects of Moody Bible Institute.

Lonnie and I moved to South Bend in the summer of 1990. At the time, for married students in academia, the conventional approach to academic life was to complete a doctorate, secure a full-time academic position with a modest but dependable salary, then start a family. We chose a more creative path, and by the time we moved to South Bend, Lonnie was four months pregnant with our first child. Fortunately, we had gotten an early start on homeowning during our second year at Michigan, when her parents cosigned a mortgage to purchase a small fixer-upper house in Ypsilanti, Ann Arbor's lower-cost neighbor to the east. With ample assistance from my father-in-law, a professional builder, we flipped the house and were able to buy an old house on Rex Street in South Bend for the laughable price, by today's standards, of $32,000. Unbeknownst to us, part of the reason for the low price was that Rex Street was a popular neighborhood for Notre Dame undergraduate house parties. After a few months of lying awake listening to all-night parties, we managed to sell the house at a profit and move to a modest ranch house in a quiet subdivision for the remainder of graduate school.

ooooo

My introduction to graduate school culture was a welcome lunch for about ten incoming students at the home of Dr. Critchlow, the director of graduate studies for the History Department. For his opening pep talk, Dr. Critchlow said, "Starting today, you're competing with graduate students at Harvard, Princeton, and elsewhere for academic jobs, so you need to start building your résumés for that goal." It was my first exposure to the reality that while learning is important, graduate school is different from undergraduate. It's essentially vocational school for academicians. Having sampled subjects during the undergraduate years and chosen the discipline of history, our task now was to leverage our graduate school experience—through research papers, attending conferences, and earning recommendations from professors—toward a career in the challenging job market of academia. In other words, college is a great opportunity to explore opportunities and develop self-awareness; in graduate school it's time to buy some sturdy work boots, assemble your toolkit, and learn the trade. While I certainly enjoyed academic life over the next six years, I never forgot that the goal was to finish the degree and get a job—a fact made even more obvious by our growing family. As the saying goes, "the best dissertation is a done dissertation."

For the first two years, however, academic life at Notre Dame was not altogether different from life at Michigan, other than the total focus on history courses that led to the master's degree. I still attended classes, but they were smaller and professors expected more work. In Dr. Nugent's weekly seminar on the history of the American West, for example, we were expected to be ready to discuss five or six books for each weekly class topic. That didn't mean reading each book cover to cover, but it did mean understanding the books' particular interpretation of the topic and their supporting evidence. I also had charismatic lecturers such as the Civil War historian Robert Kerby, who had personally visited each of the war's 384 documented battlefields. Before each class period began, Dr. Kerby filled up the chalkboard across the entire front of the room with detailed colored chalk drawings of maps, weapons, and battle formations. While modern academia tends to concern itself more with social, economic, and ideological aspects of history, Kerby was an old-school military historian who reveled in the details of the Battle of Chickamauga and who conveyed the excitement of history through words and chalk rather than PowerPoint and videos.

Of course, I had come to Notre Dame in order to make sense of my own faith by exploring the history of American evangelicalism, primarily by studying with Nathan Hatch. During my first year, he graciously hosted a small cohort of students in his office for a weekly reading group on religion in the early Republic, but his administrative duties were occupying much of his attention. (He clearly had a knack for it—soon after I left Notre Dame, Hatch was promoted to provost despite being a Protestant, and later he served as president of Wake Forest University for sixteen years.) Moreover, while a few evangelical graduate students who had come to Notre Dame before me to study with Hatch were still finishing up their doctorates, I was generally on my own as an evangelical in the graduate program, and without a professor who shared my academic interests.

In the spring of my second year, however, word began circulating that George Marsden, author of the "orange book," was planning to move on from his current position at Duke Divinity School. The two most likely landing spots were Yale University, from which Marsden had earned his PhD, and Notre Dame, which offered him an endowed chair as Francis A. McAneny Professor of History. Yale was the more prestigious institution, but Notre Dame benefited from intangible factors such as its proximity to West Michigan, where the Marsdens had a summer home on Lake Michigan, and many close personal connections stemming from their two decades at Calvin College. In addition, with the recruitment of the renowned Christian philosopher Alvin Plantinga from Calvin to Notre Dame in 1982, Notre Dame had developed a reputation for being a hospitable environment for evangelical scholars. Thus it was in the summer of 1992 that George and his wife, Lucie, arrived in South Bend, and my real graduate education began in earnest.

ooooo

George Marsden was born in 1939 in Harrisburg, Pennsylvania. His parents were active members in the Orthodox Presbyterian Church (OPC), a conservative break-off of the Northern Presbyterian Church during the fundamentalist-modernist controversies of the early 1900s. Technically, therefore, both George and I are descendants of American fundamentalism, but we come from very different branches of the tree. Whereas Moody Bible Institute arose out of revivalist, populist Christianity, the OPC emerged from the intellectual tradition of Reformed Christianity. This movement had its source with John Calvin and flowed from the English Puritans to the Ivy League institutions of colonial America, to the Presbyterian and Congregationalist colleges that dominated US higher education in the 1800s. OPC founder J. Gresham Machen, one of the theological progenitors of fundamentalism, taught at Princeton Theological Seminary before leaving to help establish Westminster Theological Seminary, where George's father was a member of the first graduating class.

Another group descending from Calvinism and sharing John Calvin's emphasis on learning was the Dutch Reformed church.

One of its pioneering thinkers was Abraham Kuyper, a turn-of-the-century Dutch Reformed theologian, politician, and founder of the Free University of Amsterdam. Kuyper advocated an approach to learning in which Christianity was integrated into all academic disciplines. As he famously put it, "There is not a square inch on the whole plain of human existence over which Christ, who is Lord over all, does not proclaim, 'This is Mine!'" For higher education, this approach meant that chemistry and sociology had as much place in the Christian college curriculum as theology and philosophy. Dutch immigrants to America founded Calvin College in 1876, and the college came to reflect the Kuyperian influence on learning. Thus from the start, Calvin College, unlike the Bible institutes, was characterized by a rigorous devotion to learning across the disciplines and a belief that the life of the mind was itself a way to worship God.

George Marsden was a product of this Reformed tradition. After earning a bachelor's degree at Haverford College, he attended the newly formed Westminster Theological Seminary before completing a doctorate in history at Yale University under the tutelage of Sydney Ahlstrom, the preeminent historian of American religion at the time. In 1965, at the age of twenty-six, he began teaching at Calvin College and soon emerged as a leading figure helping to reclaim a Christian scholarly voice in the academy. The publication of *Fundamentalism and American Culture* in 1980 established Marsden's reputation as a leading historian of American religion. In 1986, Marsden left Calvin for Duke Divinity School, and a few years later joined the faculty at Notre Dame.

With Hatch's move into administration, Marsden became the logical choice as my faculty advisor, and his personal example and mentoring over the next four years were more formative than anything else at Notre Dame. George exuded a quiet, unassuming demeanor reflected in his clothes—typically a shirt or sweater of neutral color along with baggy khaki trousers and brown shoes. His brown hair was in various levels of dishevelment, depending on the date of the last haircut, and his facial hair exuded a mentality that the next book deadline is more important than a trimmed beard.

George's cheerful, dry wit lay just below the surface of his placid exterior. It was well known that George met and started dating his wife, Lucie, when she was a student at Calvin. He liked to remark with a wry grin, "I took advantage of a brief window of opportunity between the decline of Victorian morality and the rise of political correctness." Later in my academic career, I was reading one of George's books and chuckled when I came across the word "anti-disestablishmentarianism." I knew that he was fond of the word because it was purportedly the longest nontechnical word in the English language, and although there were probably easier ways to communicate his point in the book, he had contrived to get that word in the text. Anyone who spent time with Marsden also quickly noticed his genuine sense of humility, despite his scholarly accomplishments. George and Lucie would sometimes dabble at playing the piano and flute together. George liked to tell the story of them playing in the living room when their son Greg, who became a first-rate jazz saxophonist, heard them and moaned, "Please tell me I'm adopted!"

In addition to his individual impact on students, one of George's most significant accomplishments at Notre Dame was the cultivation, along with philosopher Alvin Plantinga and others, of a Christian scholarly community. Each year, several dozen bright young Christians, many of them graduates of Christian colleges such as Calvin and Wheaton, applied to study with George, and only a handful were accepted. As their numbers grew and were augmented by Nathan Hatch's remaining students, grumblings about a "Marsden Mafia" at Notre Dame arose in certain corners of the university. The Marsdens hosted frequent gatherings for professors and graduate students at their home a few miles north of campus—Lucie the extrovert serving as the energetic host, George the introvert content to linger in the background. In addition to learning to enjoy robust intellectual conversations, I developed a Reformed Christian appreciation for God's good creation that included not only savory food but beer and wine. From George I first learned to enjoy Beck's and Amstel Light, though eventually I progressed to more substantial porters and India pale ales.

George also illustrated the fact that good teachers come in a variety of types. He talked slowly, thoughtfully, and softly, and I can't imagine students at Calvin flocking to his history lectures. As an endowed chair at Notre Dame, however, George's efforts were focused on graduate students, and it was in graduate-level seminars with small groups of students that he excelled. Although I had finished coursework by the time he arrived, I took advantage of the opportunity to attend his seminars on American fundamentalism and the history of higher education. George would typically begin the seminar with some opening questions, which would spark a discussion of the relevant text among the students. After a while, the discussion would taper off, reach an impasse, or arrive at a particularly knotty issue, and students would look to George. Then he would lean back in his chair, look up toward the ceiling, and put his hand on his head before culminating the conversation with a particular insight or a new question.

As a historian, Marsden modeled careful, methodical scholarship based in thorough research. George was an avid golfer, and one student once made the apt remark, "George writes like he golfs." George regularly outplayed his graduate students on the course by driving the fairway, avoiding bunkers, and putting consistently. His scholarship took the same approach. He was the master of qualifying words like "probably" and "somewhat" that undercut disagreement but also enabled him to subtly advance provocative new arguments—such as that fundamentalism was at heart a religious, not a social, movement; or that the modern academy unfairly privileges secular outlooks just as earlier colleges favored religious ones. Like the golfer who consistently outdrove George only to end up with a higher score at the end of the round, scholars who were not initially inclined to accept Marsden's perspective often found themselves inevitably agreeing by the end of the book.

In the early 1990s, George was working on *The Soul of the American University: From Protestant Establishment to Established Non-belief*, a dense, exhaustively researched 480-page monograph that would become one of his most important works. George would circulate chapter drafts to his seminar students to discuss, which ushered us behind the curtain of a premier scholar working at his craft. The long list of prominent scholars who were mentored by Marsden at Notre Dame includes Darren Dochuk, Kristen Du Mez, Thomas Kidd, and Steven Nolt.

As a mentor, George was kind but exacting. When he came to Notre Dame in the fall of 1992, I was preparing for doctoral comprehensive exams, which at Notre Dame consisted of extensive reading in five subject areas, followed by a written exam in each area and culminating in a combined oral exam. My main area, of course, was American religion, directed by George. I showed him a list of about one hundred titles in the field, including Sydney Ahlstrom's 1,200-page *Religious History of the American People*, hoping that he would narrow the list down for me. His reply was, "Yes, that looks like what a scholar of American religion should be familiar with." George's supervisory role in my case, however, was made more complicated by the fact that he took piano lessons from my wife, Lonnie. Thus, while I was studying and writing a dissertation for George, at least I could take comfort in hearing Lonnie kindly but firmly remind him that he needed to work more on his left hand. Our friendship with George and Lucie began during those years and continues three decades later.

∞∞∞

As far as school itself was concerned, my next few years were a nearly monk-like existence—one year preparing for and taking doctoral exams, followed by two years of researching and writing a dissertation. Around the outside walls of Notre Dame's fourteen-story library are a few hundred small, locked carrels that serve as tiny offices for graduate students. In my second year there, I was fortunate to acquire a carrel on the thirteenth floor, one of the few that had a window. The south wall of the library faces the football stadium and contains the iconic mural of Touchdown Jesus, and so I could conveniently inform people that my carrel was just below Jesus's right armpit. On weekdays, I would arrive at the library at 7:30 a.m. and take the elevator up to the thirteenth floor—sometimes accompanied by President Hesburgh, whose office occupied the fourteenth floor—and work in my carrel until departing for home at 5:30 p.m. The routine was broken up by a daily lunch hour with other graduate students in the library basement and a freshman US history class for which I was the teaching assistant.

My work regimen stemmed partly from a stubborn, task-oriented personality, but also from my life situation. Five months into my first year at Notre Dame, Ryan was born. Fifteen months later, Tyler came on the scene, and two and a half years later, our daughter Rachel joined the team. However attractive the life of the mind may have seemed, the life of an employed person took priority. During the academic year, I earned a modest graduate student stipend as a teaching assistant while Lonnie gave piano lessons and taught part time in Notre Dame's music department.

The real earnings occurred in the summer: I had helped a friend paint an old house back in Ann Arbor, and concluding that this qualified me to be a house painter, I operated a painting business, creatively titled Rick's Painting, from late May to late August. An old Moody friend, Dave Lunow, owned a rusty Toyota pickup truck, and together we spent the summer months driving our ladders and equipment around the neighborhoods of South Bend scraping, priming, and painting old houses. An old Celtic prayer states, "Labor and rest, work and ease; the busy hand, and then the skilled thought. This blending of opposites is the secret of the joy of living." The Celtic monks may have blended working and thinking daily; in my case, it was nine months of academic work punctuated by three months of manual labor. And while I didn't find it to be the secret of the joy of living, along with some school loans, it did get Lonnie and me and our growing family through graduate school.

I didn't realize it at the time, but in promoting my business, bidding jobs, dealing with customers, and taking pride in quality work, my summer employment ultimately constituted an important part of my graduate school education. While academicians resist calling students "customers" and bristle at comparing a college to a business, the difference should not be overstated: we have a service to sell (education), and we're only in business if we find buyers and provide a satisfying experience. And while the "deliverables" in academia may not be as visible as a freshly painted house, both the painter and the educator depend on the customer's trust in their competence and integrity. Just as the university can mask, at least for a time, subpar academics with climbing walls and gourmet dishes, so a fresh coat of paint can cover a poorly prepared surface, only to peel off in next year's summer heat. In my subsequent career as an academic administrator, lessons from the painting business frequently came to mind.

During my third year at Notre Dame studying beneath Jesus's armpit, I managed to pass comprehensive exams in April, which left me with one more assignment—a three-hundred-page history dissertation. My chosen topic was a history of changing Protestant views of prayer in the late 1800s and early 1900s in response to the rise of modern science, for which I borrowed a book title from that era: "The Life of Prayer in a World of Science." I had an interesting topic, as dissertations go, and a strong work ethic, but I still had much to learn as a Christian scholar. Part of my subject matter dealt with liberal Protestants, and in particular their views of prayer and spirituality. As an evangelical Christian who had been conditioned to view liberal Protestantism with suspicion, I had difficulty taking liberal Protestant spirituality seriously and was generally dismissive of their attempt to reenvision prayer in new ways. Eighteen months into my dissertation project, my research basically complete, I submitted a rough draft for George to review. The result was a three-page letter that is etched vividly in my mind. In his gentle but firm way, George essentially said, "You have a long way to go with this project because you're not taking your subjects seriously. You're reading liberal Protestant writings on prayer from your evangelical perspective, and as a result you're not telling a true story about the past because you haven't learned to take your subjects on their own terms." After years of study, it was a sobering experience. I sat on a bench along the campus lake on a beautiful sunny afternoon, wondering whether I had wasted the past five years of my life.

In retrospect, George was teaching the same lesson I learned from Dr. Walton years earlier at Moody: a key quality of a scholar is humility—the ability to submit ourselves and our preconceptions to the subject, whether that's the Bible or a science experiment, and pay attention to what it is telling us. Essentially, George was reprimanding me for doing the same thing with liberal Protestant writings on prayer that Walton's fundamentalist counterparts had done—failing to get outside of my own preconceptions and really pay attention to what the data was telling me. And for George, taking the data seriously was central to who we are as Christian scholars. The flaw in my project was not in the research but in my orientation toward the data. Fortunately, with some coaching from my mentor, that was an easier problem to fix than doing more research. After rewriting those chapters and completing the manuscript, I was able to successfully defend my dissertation by the spring of 1996, and a few years later Oxford University Press published it as a book.

∞∞∞∞

In the spring of 1996, therefore, with a wife and three young children and my dissertation nearing completion, just one task remained: finding a job. Of course, as Dr. Critchlow had pointed out several years earlier, that's what those graduate students at Harvard, Yale, and Princeton—and a hundred other universities—were doing as well. Since my goal was to find a position at a teaching-oriented college or university, it was important to get some actual teaching experience on the résumé. Fortunately, that spring, Taylor University in Upland, Indiana, had three course vacancies at its Fort Wayne campus. Another Marsden student, Jay Case, and I were hired to teach the classes. Unfortunately, Fort Wayne is two hours away from South Bend. Thus, every Monday, Wednesday, and Friday at 5:30 a.m., Jay and I would carpool to Fort Wayne, teach our classes, and return by dinnertime. I taught US history, which I knew well, and world history, which I didn't, and which required staying four pages ahead of the students in the textbook's sections on the Gupta Empire and the Han Dynasty. Taking the work might have seemed crazy, but it was an opportunity to grab the first rung of the academic ladder, and so Jay and I took it. Moreover, in today's challenging academic market, it's the rung occupied by about

700,000 college teachers, or nearly 40 percent of the total faculty workforce in the United States. Ask any adjunct professor in a large metropolitan area who is cobbling courses together to make ends meet, and they'll likely tell you that they spend as much time in their car as in the classroom.

Even with two courses on my résumé, my job prospects looked bleak as I sent off one application letter after another. One small Catholic college in the Northeast stated in their rejection letter that there were over 350 applicants for the position. During the job search, my father-in-law wondered aloud to Lonnie whether I wasn't better off sticking with my painting business in South Bend, which would have been an ironic but not unprecedented use of a doctoral degree in the humanities. Fortunately I belonged to a subcommunity of academia, evangelical higher education, where the combination of Moody, Michigan, and Marsden carried some appeal. I applied for an opening at Greenville University in southern Illinois, made it through the early search stages, and was invited to campus in March.

Greenville is a typical small Christian liberal arts college. With campus buildings dating from the 1850s, it sits adjacent to the quiet town of Greenville and its five thousand residents. Lonnie and I stayed overnight in the old campus guest house and spent a day visiting with faculty and administrators, and I gave a guest lecture to a group of students and faculty. All of the signals seemed positive, and as we drove back to South Bend, I thought, "So this is the happy ending after years studying and painting houses. I'll teach history at Greenville, Lonnie will work in the music department, and we'll raise our family in southern Illinois." A couple of days later, I received a phone call from the search committee chair. The committee was generally positive, he said, but they would like to see a video of me actually teaching a class. Did I have something I could send them? I didn't have a video, but I borrowed a camera from Notre Dame, lugged it to Fort Wayne, and set it up in the back of the classroom to record my US history class.

Before sending the video off to Greenville, I watched it myself and was taken aback at the contrast between the perception of the classroom from inside my head and the reality captured by the video camera. What I thought was a witty, eloquent lecture was essentially forty-five minutes of pacing back and forth in front of a roomful of bored students, droning on about the topic while sprinkling my delivery with a few dozen "uhs" and "ums." Graduate programs today generally do a better job of cultivating their students as teachers as well as researchers, but in the 1990s, even quality programs such as Notre Dame generally seemed to assume that if doctoral students read enough books and did enough research, somehow they would also develop some skill at what for most of them will compose the vast majority of their professional time—teaching. Unfortunately for me, it was not until my last semester of graduate school, and in the thick of a job search, that I first saw myself in action and realized how much I needed to grow to be an effective college teacher, whether at Greenville or anywhere else. I mailed the video and hoped that the committee would at least perceive a kernel of potential tucked away somewhere in my lecture.

At about the same time, another Christian college announced an opening in history. It was a small, financially struggling Southern Baptist institution that called itself Grand Canyon University, even though it was actually located in Phoenix, about two hundred miles from the South Rim of the canyon. Once again I applied and eventually received an invitation for a campus visit, though the school couldn't afford to invite Lonnie out with me. While still far from a master teacher, I had at least learned enough from watching my video to know that I had to refine my delivery, up my energy level, and, as advised by Jay Parini's *The Art of Teaching*, come across as a more vibrant version of my typical introverted self.

The method worked, and a few days after my visit, I received a phone call offering me a tenure-track position with a modest starting salary of $28,000. In the meantime, Greenville was still in the deliberation process, which left us with the decision whether to wait on Greenville or take the Grand Canyon offer. From our experiences at Moody, Lonnie and I had formed a commitment that we would not let money or location dictate our decisions in life but would go wherever we believed God was leading us. Coupled with this principle has been a tendency to favor the new and unknown—"when in doubt, take the more adventurous option"— which in this case definitely favored Phoenix's desert landscape over the cornfields of southern Illinois. True to form, Lonnie, who had never set foot in the Southwest, remarked, "Let's go to Arizona." The Kawai was in for its longest trip yet.

ooooo

Working on a PhD while starting a family is not an experience that I would recommend for everyone, but I did gain some valuable lessons from my Notre Dame years, even though to this day I can't bring myself to root for their football team. First, by participating in a community of scholars that included Hatch, Marsden, and Plantinga, I was able to witness firsthand a healthy blend of piety and intellect. Bible college evangelicals have sometimes believed that scholarly excellence comes at the expense of spiritual devotion, but that suspicion for me was dispelled at Notre Dame. Anyone who has spent ample time with George will recall his prayers before meals or at public gatherings. He typically begins with an interval of silence that borders on awkwardness, then embarks on an eloquent, humble prayer that expresses a deep spirituality matching his scholarly excellence. After my time at Notre Dame, Marsden went on to write what is probably his culminating work, *Jonathan Edwards: A Life*, in which he showed, among other things, that love for God could inspire a powerful and wide-ranging intellect. While certainly there are examples of anti-intellectual piety and spiritually arid rationalism, it has always been apparent to me that healthy Christian academic communities can love God with both heart and mind, and I have Notre Dame to thank for that.

Second, it's not a coincidence that the vigorous approach to integrating Christian faith and scholarship that I witnessed at Notre Dame came through the specific vehicle of Reformed Protestantism. Years later, when I wrote a book on Christian higher education for college students, I was accused by some of subtly promoting a Reformed version of Christianity. While it's probably true that I display something of the zeal of the adult convert to the

Reformed vision of education, it's also difficult to envision a robust approach to integrating faith and learning that doesn't employ the creation-fall-redemption paradigm articulated by Calvin, Kuyper, and many others in the Reformed tradition. There seems to be something in the "transformationist" vision of Reformed Christianity and its emphasis on Christ's lordship over every aspect of creation that fosters rigorous and consciously Christian scholarship. While other legitimate models of Christian higher education exist, such as Anabaptist, Lutheran, and Quaker, it's difficult to imagine other Protestant traditions creating a flourishing subcommunity at Notre Dame the way that Reformed scholars have done.

Third, for all of the challenges of combining full-time graduate school with starting a family, I benefited immeasurably from the opportunity to spend a stage of life immersing myself in a scholarly community. Many higher-education professionals are forced to chip away at a doctorate for years while working full time in a college or church. While that may be a necessity, like watching *Star Wars* on an iPhone, doing so lacks the full sensory experience. Beyond the coursework, papers, and exams, graduate school essentially is a multi-year apprenticeship and induction into the world of a professional academic. Despite the struggles, I'm grateful for a season of life in which I could live and breathe my dissertation and be mentored by a rigorous and patient scholar. The graduate school experience is far from perfect—some apprenticeship in teaching would have been particularly valuable in my case—but it is an immersive experience that forms individuals as scholars and cannot be replicated by other means. Many of the debates within universities between professors and nonprofessors, I suspect, stem from the uniquely formative role that full-time graduate school plays in a professor's life.

Finally, I'm grateful that my graduate school experience ultimately led to an actual job in academia, albeit one that paid considerably less at the outset than I could have made painting houses. Such an outcome is increasingly rare in US higher education. A 2020 National Science Foundation survey of 19,500 PhD recipients in 2020 found that only 40 percent of them had secured positions in academe.[5] Obviously that number reflects the financially stressed nature of many colleges and universities and the further outsourcing of faculty work to part-time employees. It also reflects the fact that in many fields, one can earn significantly more in industry than in academia, and for PhDs with families to support, sometimes the economic considerations are unavoidable. Full-time professors who have been shaped by the graduate school experience can be quirky, impractical, and opinionated; as an administrator, I have had my fair share of faculty-induced headaches over the years. But such scholars also form the core of our institutions and ultimately their work with students is what college is about. The future flourishing of higher education depends on maintaining a healthy supply of full-time, graduate school–trained professors.

oooooo

DESERT INTERLUDE

If Lonnie and I were looking for something different from the Midwest, Phoenix in mid-August did not disappoint. My father and I drove a U-Haul truck with our Ford Taurus station wagon in tow across the country and arrived in Phoenix on a 113-degree day. Lonnie flew to Phoenix sight-unseen with three small children, walked out of Sky Harbor International Airport, and experienced the typical visitor's impression of stepping into an oven. We moved into a small bungalow on the north side of Phoenix, and I began my first college teaching job at Grand Canyon University.

oooooo

Grand Canyon College was founded in 1949 by Arizona Southern Baptists in Prescott, Arizona, with sixteen professors and one hundred students. Two years later, the college moved to a ninety-acre tract in West Phoenix. It gained accreditation in 1968 and became a university in 1989. Other than a successful baseball program that placed some alums in the major leagues, Grand Canyon University (GCU) was little known in the world of higher education until 2004, when it was sold to California-based Significant Education and became the first for-profit Christian university in the United States. New online programs quickly emerged, and by 2018, with twenty thousand on-campus students and another seventy thousand online, GCU billed itself as the world's largest Christian university.

The Grand Canyon that I joined in the fall of 1996 gave little indication of such a destiny. Throughout its five decades as a private Southern Baptist institution, the university struggled to compete for students against more prominent Christian competitors in Southern California such as Azusa Pacific and Biola. Competing with regional public institutions such as Arizona State University, GCU was forced to keep its tuition unusually low for a private university.

The anthropologist Clifford Geertz, in an essay on academia, coined what he called the "exile from Eden syndrome" among academicians. Most professors, he noted, typically begin their academic careers at major research universities, then end up at schools that are, he said, "lower down or further out."[6] Coming from Notre Dame, the "exile from Eden" motif seemed appropriate to me, both geographically and institutionally. Like a large family subsisting for years on a meager paycheck, GCU's campus showed the effects of its cash-strapped status, from unkept green spaces to offices housed in trailers with small window-unit air conditioners working feverishly to combat the desert heat. The contrast with Notre Dame's immaculate campus and landmark buildings such as the Golden Dome could not have been starker.

I was joined by another tenure-track humanities hire, a new philosophy PhD from Emory University named Douglas Henry. Despite its financial hardships, the university sought to treat us well. We had private offices, and the dean, Robin Baker, scraped professional development funds together to enable me to attend an academic conference in my first year. As is typically the case at private universities, however, the teaching load was challenging, both in the number of courses and size of the classes. In my first semester, I taught two sections of US History I to classes of about ninety students each, a smaller class of US History II, and an upper-level course in colonial history. I was certainly not the Francis A. McAneny Chair of History waxing eloquent to a handful of doctoral students.

As an undergraduate at Michigan, I had watched Russell Fraser orchestrate class discussions on Shakespeare for over a hundred students seemingly with effortless ease. I was not Russell Fraser and this was not Michigan, however, so I took a less adventurous path and tried to cobble together interesting lectures. After my first essay exam produced a formidable tower of ungraded blue books on my desk, I resorted to overly complicated multiple-choice exams that at least gave me the sense that I was being academically rigorous by quizzing students on the minutiae of American history.

In general, the fall semester went tolerably well. Then one day in early January, I was in my office preparing for class when Lonnie called and uttered the attention-grabbing words, "Are you sitting down?" before informing me that she was pregnant with child number four. My modest salary and Lonnie's piano lesson income were already stretched to the breaking point to support a family of five, and recently the air-conditioning had gone out in our old Ford Taurus station wagon—not a good thing in Phoenix. The numbers weren't working out.

The numbers weren't working for Grand Canyon University either. During the winter, Robin Baker was engaged in lengthy deliberations with the university's administrators and board members about how to keep the university financially solvent. The situation was further complicated by the school's prominent athletic programs, which boosted the institution's public profile but had voracious financial appetites. To his credit, although having just hired a PhD from Notre Dame, Robin nevertheless informed me of the university's situation and suggested that it might be best for my growing family to find a position at a more stable institution. He even had a specific school to suggest—John Brown University (JBU) in Siloam Springs, Arkansas—where he had taught history for two years before returning to his alma mater in Phoenix.

A more stable university sounded good, but John Brown University was not exactly what I had in mind. As a native Chicagoan, I harbored the typical northerner stereotypes about Arkansas. Also, the school's name sounded a lot like Bob Jones University, and given its location in Arkansas, I assumed that John Brown shared Bob Jones's strict fundamentalist orientation. Robin, however, assured me that it was a broadly evangelical institution and might be a good fit for Lonnie and me. I applied for the history position there and received an invitation to interview on campus.

In 1997, northwest Arkansas had no regional airport to speak of. Visitors typically flew into Tulsa, Oklahoma, rented a car, and drove seventy-five miles across northeast Oklahoma on the Cherokee Turnpike. After passing the Cherokee Casino and some liquor stores bunched on the western border of Benton County, Arkansas—which had become a dry county decades earlier thanks to the efforts of John Brown Sr.—one arrived in Siloam Springs. Lonnie and I made the journey on a Saturday evening in February. The next morning, we drove around town looking for a Denny's or a Cracker Barrel in order to eat breakfast before attending a local church. Finding none, we settled on Braum's, which is essentially a southern equivalent to Dairy Queen with a slightly larger menu. As Lonnie and I sat in a booth eating pancakes off Styrofoam plates with plastic forks, a rusty blue church bus drove by with "Liberty Baptist Church" emblazoned across the side. We looked at each other and chuckled.

Later that day and the next, however, we met a variety of interesting and competent people who enjoyed the work of Christian higher education. The president, Lee Balzer, was a former dean of natural sciences at Seattle Pacific University, a reputable Christian university in the Northwest. The chair of the History Department, Ed Ericson, was a graduate of Calvin College and earned his PhD from Indiana University. His father, a noted Solzhenitsyn scholar, had been a fellow faculty member with George Marsden at Calvin. Then there was the friendly Texan Terri Wubbena, chair of the Music Department, and her husband, Jan Helmut Wubbena, an intense German pipe organ virtuoso who taught rigorous courses on music history and theory. By the end of our visit, despite the inauspicious start, we concluded that JBU might be a place where we could enjoy working. A couple of weeks later, the chair of the search committee called and offered me the position.

ooooo

Grand Canyon University was a valuable learning experience for a new PhD coming out of Notre Dame. Whatever the merits of Geertz's "exiles from Eden" analogy, I discovered that highly qualified, dedicated people are embedded throughout the landscape of private higher education. Douglas Henry stayed at Grand Canyon one year longer than me, then left for Malone University and eventually joined Baylor University, where he now serves as dean of the Honors College. Robin Baker continued to lead the attempt to keep Grand Canyon solvent and operating until he left in 1999 to become provost at George Fox University. He became president there in 2007 and continues in that role. Many others have faithfully continued to serve at Grand Canyon despite the decades of turmoil surrounding the university's transition to a large for-profit institution. Jim Helfers, for example, a graduate of Wheaton College who earned his PhD at Michigan, served as a mentor in my first year and has faithfully taught English at GCU for thirty years. I even taught a particularly bright history major, Trisha Posey, who would someday be hired to replace me at John Brown University and who serves today as director of JBU's Honors Scholars Program. Such examples of competent and dedicated professionals abound throughout private higher education.

I also learned that while educational ideals are great, colleges need sufficient resources and a solid financial model in order to accomplish what they are created to do. As someone once remarked, "no margin, no mission." Maslow's hierarchy of needs posits that individuals must have their basic physiological and safety needs met before they can grow cognitively and aesthetically and pursue self-actualization. Whatever the merits of Maslow's hierarchy for individuals, institutions that consume so much time and energy making ends meet from one year to the next do have little margin to explore new educational approaches or consider how they might achieve their mission more effectively. In today's challenging environment for private colleges and universities, there are many institutions whose situations resemble Grand Canyon in the late 1990s, and I have visited several of them. Few have taken the drastic step of becoming a for-profit online institution, but some resort to mergers, a few close their doors each year, and many others slog on. Whatever the outcome, operating at the subsistence level is not conducive to achieving quality higher education.

For Lonnie and me and our growing family, however, it was time to move on to a more stable institution, even if that meant relocating to a town of ten thousand in the Bible Belt of northwest Arkansas. So, in July, having laid our Taurus station wagon to rest, we packed our minivan and left the desert heat of Phoenix for the green hills of the Ozarks.

ooooo

FOUR

Loosening the Bible Belt

W E ARRIVED IN SILOAM SPRINGS, Arkansas, in August 1997. Lonnie, eight months pregnant and adaptable as always, unpacked our new house on Mount Olive Street, went to the hospital in the early hours of September 5, and Anna was born before breakfast. So began our twelve years at John Brown University. The loaded question at our visits up north, "So how long are you going to live in Arkansas?" gradually subsided as the years went by. Lonnie embarked on a productive career in the Music Department, teaching piano and accompanying individuals and ensembles. She also served as the wise older sister to stressed-out music majors, some of whom would occasionally break down during a rehearsal and sit beside her on the piano bench for a long conversation. I spent six years as a faculty member, six more years as a dean, and forged many of my fondest personal and professional memories at the school.

ooooo

In order to understand the significance of my time at John Brown University, we need to briefly return to my time at Notre Dame. In 1993, Wheaton College launched a search for a new president, and Notre Dame's Nathan Hatch had the perfect résumé. He was a Wheaton alum, a first-rate scholar with a PhD from Washington University, a significant public intellectual, and had a proven record as an administrator at Notre Dame. Since the 1950s, evangelical colleges, emerging from the shadow of fundamentalism, were developing as quality academic institutions with a commitment to "Christian faith integration." Calvin College, with its first-rate faculty such as George Marsden and Alvin Plantinga, played an important role in that process, but so too did Wheaton. Founded in 1860 and known within evangelicalism as the "Fundamentalist Harvard," Wheaton boasted one of the oldest pedigrees among Christian colleges and considered itself the flagship evangelical college. For evangelical intellectuals, the selection of Nathan Hatch to lead Wheaton to new academic heights seemed a natural choice.

Wheaton's board of trustees, however, didn't see it that way. Christian colleges have always had two voices whispering in their ears—one encouraging them toward greater intellectual respectability, the other warning of creeping liberalism, especially among the faculty, and a loss of spiritual fervor. Harvard, after all, started as a Puritan college, and look at it now. Heeding the second voice, Wheaton's leadership bypassed Hatch and selected Duane Litfin as president. His résumé, while also distinguished, was markedly different from Hatch's: Litfin earned his undergraduate degree at Philadelphia College of the Bible (a sister school to Moody Bible Institute), had a master's degree from Dallas Theological Seminary, and was pastoring a church in Memphis, Tennessee, when Wheaton called.

Evangelical scholars were scandalized, some literally. Wheaton College historian Mark Noll, a friend of Hatch and Marsden, subsequently wrote *The Scandal of the Evangelical Mind*. Named by *Christianity Today* as Book of the Year for 1995, *Scandal* summarized the outlook of a generation of evangelical scholars. It became standard reading for Christian graduate students and for just about anyone else in Christian higher education at the time. Deep in the American evangelical DNA, Noll lamented, lay a populist, pragmatic, anti-intellectual streak that has undermined scholarship and impeded the creation of first-rate evangelical academic institutions. "The scandal of the evangelical mind," he began, "is that there is not much of an evangelical mind."[7] Noll's most scathing chapter, "The Intellectual Disaster of Fundamentalism," chronicled the effects of early twentieth-century fundamentalism on evangelical ideas and institutions of the late twentieth century. *Scandal* became the lens through which young evangelical scholars of my generation viewed their efforts and institutions.

ooooo

Few Christian universities bore the imprint of fundamentalism more than John Brown University. Its name actually derives not from the famous abolitionist but from an early twentieth-century traveling evangelist who was deeply connected to the fundamentalist movement. John Elward Brown grew up in rural Iowa and was converted to Christianity at a Salvation Army revival meeting while traveling through Arkansas. He became an itinerant evangelist in the early 1900s and was known as one of several "Billy Sundays of the South" during the era. Later Brown moved to Southern California to launch a radio station and Christian schools that blended Christian values and patriotism. Two decades later, when Billy Graham became a celebrity evangelist through his Los Angeles tour, John Brown was one of the key figures promoting his revivals.

In 1919, concluding that poor, rural young people would benefit from an education that fused Christian truth and practical training in skilled trades, John Brown founded Southwestern College on his family farm in the northwest Arkansas town of Siloam Springs. Among the communities that might lay claim to the title of "Buckle of the Bible Belt," Siloam Springs would certainly merit consideration. Roughly equidistant from Dallas, Oklahoma City, Kansas City, and Little Rock, the town is reported to have the highest number of churches per capita in the United States. Whether the actual buckle or not, Siloam Springs was fertile soil for a college blending conservative religion, practical education, and Christian patriotism.

In addition to providing tuition-free vocational training, Southwestern was meant to be an antidote to the secularism that was rampant in universities and that was turning out, according to Brown, students who "specialized in nothing, unless it is cigarette smoking, athletics, and the Charleston."[8] Unable to raise sufficient funds to provide tuition-free education, the college began charging modest tuition in its early years, but it has continued to keep its tuition lower than most private institutions. Moreover, the university has maintained its vocational emphasis through programs such as Construction Management and Engineering.

After John Brown's death in 1957, JBU moved away from strict fundamentalism, a shift symbolized in 1969 when it hosted Billy Graham on campus. Theologically, however, the university remained fundamentalist both in its theological orientation and in imposing strict moral codes for students. Until the 1990s, its Bible Department was largely recruited from dispensationalist institutions such as Dallas Seminary. Also, for its first seventy years, the university was run essentially as a family business. In 1948, John Brown appointed his son, John Brown Jr., as president but remained chair of the board. In 1979, John Brown Jr. was succeeded as president by John Brown III.

Despite its fundamentalist heritage, by the 1990s, JBU was poised to make significant progress as an evangelical university. Unlike most religious colleges in the South, JBU was from the start intentionally interdenominational. This meant that it was more open to northern evangelical influences than regional peers such as Ouachita Baptist University and Harding University. For example, David Brisben, a Presbyterian who had earned his PhD from Trinity Evangelical Divinity School in Chicago, joined the Bible faculty in 1992. His Reformed theological orientation exerted a steady influence on the theological direction and hiring of the university, especially when he became chair of the Bible Department in the late 1990s. Also, as mentioned earlier, Robin Baker had come to JBU from Wheaton College before leaving for Grand Canyon University, and my colleague in the History Department, Ed Ericson, was a Calvin graduate and the son of a Calvin professor.

Also, JBU's leadership changed in the 1990s. In 1993, John Brown III stepped down as president to make way for a non-Brown leader. After a rocky nine-month presidency by Brown's immediate successor, Lee Balzer was named president in 1994. A former dean at Seattle Pacific University and president of Tabor College in Kansas, Balzer brought an outsider's perspective and professional academic expertise to university administration. Of course, high academic aspirations count for little without resources, and JBU was well positioned financially to take a significant step forward. The first two Browns had cultivated a strong financial foundation buttressed by oil money in Texas and Oklahoma, including a significant endowment from the Chapman Charitable Trust in Tulsa. Then in the 1980s, a small network of five-and-dime stores called Walmart sprang up down the road from JBU in Bentonville, which revolutionized the economy of northwest Arkansas. Some Walmart money inevitably trickled down to JBU, and the relationship between the two organizations was strengthened when Walmart chief operating officer Don Soderquist became chair of the JBU Board of Trustees in 1995. Thus, Lee Balzer was able to leverage JBU's substantial financial and fund-raising potential to significantly expand the university's facilities, personnel, and programs.

In joining John Brown University in 1997, therefore, I had stumbled onto a university with fundamentalist origins that was nevertheless poised to become a leading evangelical university in the mold of Calvin and Wheaton. Indeed, one could view JBU as a perfect test case in the ability of evangelical higher education to overcome the "scandal" of anti-intellectualism described in detail by Mark Noll. I occupied a front-row seat, and some would say a primary role, in that story. Whether that role was hero or villain depends on whom you ask.

ooooo

My first few years at JBU, however, were spent picking up from where I left off at Grand Canyon University and learning the trade of a small college professor, which primarily means teaching. Anyone who has not experienced the daily grind of teaching four classes each semester cannot understand the mental and emotional energy continually expended in preparing class sessions, delivering lectures (especially for introverts), recovering from lectures, creating exams, grading exams and papers, and so on. Except between semesters, one is never entirely free from the nagging thought that one should be doing something to prepare for the next class or grading a stack of papers. Those professors who spend an entire career teaching and continually investing themselves in the same classes year after year are the true heroes of higher education.

I was never an outstanding teacher, but I read my course evaluations diligently and worked hard to improve. Being a visual learner myself, I tried to make history as image-based as possible. Doing so before PowerPoint and Google Images was like communicating by letter writing before email—we all did it, but looking back now, it seems incredibly inefficient. I inherited an office from my predecessor in the History Department, and among the leftover belongings was a rectangular wooden case entitled "Western Civilization Slide Collection," which contained hundreds of color slides organized by historical period. This became my treasure trove. For each class, I would select relevant slides—a map tracing Alexander the Great's conquests, images of the *Bayeux Tapestry*, grainy photos of the Battle of Stalingrad—and insert them into a carousel slide projector for use during class. Historical eras were labeled by letter and individual slides by number, so my lecture notes looked like the record of a *Battleship* board game, peppered with bold font indicators such as A-12, C-3, H-16, and the like. The images did seem to keep students more engaged, though the projector's softly whirring fan could also function as a sleep-inducing aid, especially in the class after lunch.

As the resident American historian in a two-professor department, my main course at JBU was American Studies. Strangely enough, this course vividly illustrated the tensions of late twentieth-century evangelical higher education, as conservative colleges hired young professors like me formed by the "scandal of the evangelical mind" paradigm. The typical four-year traditional undergraduate program consists of about one-third general education, one-third major, and one-third everything else (a minor, electives, study abroad, etc.). Most universities pack their general education courses into the first two years, while students are trying out different options for majors, so that students can focus on their major and minor fields during the junior and senior years. John Brown University, however, admirably maintained what it called a "developmental core curriculum" that included required nonmajor courses throughout a student's four-year career. Thus, JBU students took an unusual triad of senior-level core classes—Capstone Seminar in Christian Life, Masterpieces of Literature, and American Studies.

Why American Studies? The answer lies in the Walton Scholars Program, which funded scholarships for about sixty Central American students at the university. As Communism spread to Central America in the 1980s, Walmart founder Sam Walton created a program to identify future leaders in the region and provide them with a free college education in Arkansas (at Harding University, John Brown, or University of the Ozarks), with the stipulation that they must return to their home country for a minimum of five years after completion of their degree. The program was intended not just to provide a college education but to instill in these students a devotion to democracy and free enterprise that they would take back with them to Central America. Hence the required American Studies course, whose purpose was to promote an understanding of and respect for US political and economic values.

No one at JBU, however, informed me of the original purpose of American Studies when it became a central part of my teaching load. I was simply told to choose a topic in American history that interested me. That was easy, since my reason for studying history in the first place had been to help make sense of my American evangelical faith. Thus, the class became essentially an opportunity to expose students to the themes of *The Scandal of the Evangelical Mind* and show them how the study of religious history relativizes Christian faith, but hopefully deepens it as well.

For example, since this was the era in which conservative evangelicals began promoting a myth of America's Christian origins, our opening text for the course was *The Search for Christian America*, a book cowritten in 1989 by Nathan Hatch, George Marsden, and Mark Noll, which sought to combat that myth. The next text was Harold Frederic's 1896 novel, *The Damnation of Theron Ware*, about a devout Methodist minister who encounters Darwinian evolution and biblical higher criticism and loses his faith. The story hit uncomfortably close to home for many students whose courses at JBU in biology and biblical interpretation posed difficult questions for them, and it sparked vigorous discussions.

Next we read *Summer for the Gods: The Scopes Trial and America's Continuing Debate over Science and Religion* (1998), a book about the Scopes monkey trial and the rise of fundamentalist anti-evolutionism, which was yet another lesson in how supposedly "biblical" beliefs can arise from particular cultural situations. The course concluded with Randall Balmer's *Mine Eyes Have Seen the Glory: A Journey into the Evangelical Subculture in America* (1990). Balmer is a graduate of an evangelical college who tends to view traditional evangelicalism with a jaundiced eye. His personal story, which he weaves into the text, resonated with many of my students. Mark Noll would have loved the course; Sam Walton, probably not so much.

Twenty years in the rearview mirror, two aspects of American Studies stand out. First, for all their importance to the origins of the course, the Walton students unfortunately did not figure prominently in my planning of the course. In the late 1990s, US Christian colleges in general were just beginning to take diversity seriously. Because of the Walton program, JBU was more diverse than most Christian colleges in the Bible Belt. But apart from a few significant exceptions, especially in the Business Department, our pedagogy and faculty development programs had not caught up to our reality. The Walton students were smart and hardworking, and they generally did well in my course. But I doubt that much of the material in the course resonated with them on a personal or spiritual level. It would have made sense to incorporate topics such as the development of Hispanic Christianity in the United States, or Christian influences on US policy in Central America, but doing so didn't occur to me at the time. Ironically, a few years later, I helped to coordinate a faculty workshop on globalizing the curriculum, though I seemed unaware of the need to first "Central Americanize" my own courses to reflect the diversity that already existed. Generally speaking, evangelical educators of the 1990s were so focused on overcoming the scandal of anti-intellectualism that we overlooked the scandal of homogeneity.

Second, while using history to critique one's faith is important and doing so resonated with many of my students, like professors in general, I tended to project my own intellectual and spiritual journey onto my students. Evangelical scholars of my generation, reared in the shadow of fundamentalism, generally moved from a childhood of believing in too many absolutes to holding fewer beliefs in college years. As such, they tended to view college as a time in which students needed to have their beliefs critiqued, deconstructed, and reduced to a few essentials. While questioning one's beliefs remains an important aspect of college, I suspect that for many college students today, Christian or otherwise, the primary challenge is to arrive at *any* absolute truths that merit their firm belief and lifelong commitment in the first place. If I were still teaching the course today, along with showing the historically conditioned aspects of our faith, I would also emphasize that there are truths worth basing one's life on, and one purpose of college is to identify those truths and cultivate practices that conform our lives to those truths.

∞∞∞

While teaching constituted my main role at JBU, I also sought to maintain some semblance of the scholarly life that I had learned in graduate school. Indeed, a key component of overcoming the "scandal of the evangelical mind" was for professors not just to teach courses but, as Marsden, Plantinga, and others had done earlier at Calvin, to advance a Christian scholarly presence in the larger academy. Thus, younger professors like me who came from PhD programs saw scholarship as an important part of our work. Because of the heavy teaching load, however, significant scholarly work was primarily relegated to the unpaid summer months.

Through fortuitous timing, my primary scholarly work at John Brown University combined the themes of Noll and Marsden with the university itself. Like many evangelical institutions, JBU had paid little attention to its own historical development. An adulatory biography of the founder existed, and decades earlier a JBU professor had written a doctoral dissertation on the early years of the college. No one, however, had ever traced the development of the institution or attempted to place it within the larger context of twentieth-century evangelicalism. Having spent the early 1990s under the tutelage of George Marsden while he was completing *The Soul of the American University*, such a project was ideal for me, and some summer funding from President Balzer was icing on the cake. At the time, the university archives was an unregulated Wild West of old student newspapers, Board of Trustees minutes and correspondence, notes from cabinet meetings, and personal correspondence of the Browns and other family members. I had free run of the place, and I sought to emulate my former mentor's critical but generous approach. The result was *Head, Heart, and Hand: John Brown University and Twentieth Century Evangelical Higher Education*, published by University of Arkansas Press in 2003.

Writing a history of one's own institution, however, is tricky. The late twentieth century was also a time in which colleges and universities were beginning to come to grips with racial aspects of their past. As a historian writing a book about an originally all-white college founded in Arkansas in the early 1900s, I could not ignore the underlying role of race in the college's history. The challenge was to do so in a way that was honest and accurate but also properly contextualized and that didn't throw the founder or the school under the (segregated) bus. In a few pages of chapter 4, I showed that John Brown Sr. shared racial views that were typical of white fundamentalists of the day—views that I described as "racial separationist." Brown never endorsed white supremacist groups such as the Ku Klux Klan, which was a significant cultural force in the 1920s, but in his evangelistic campaigns he implicitly acknowledged the segregated nature of southern society by setting aside a Sunday morning service for African Americans.

Concerning the college, the sources clearly demonstrated that the founder envisioned it as a school for white students. Referring to Booker T. Washington's Tuskegee Institute, a well-known vocational college for black students, John Brown Sr. remarked that he had established John Brown University as a white counterpart to Washington's—established, he said, for "sons and daughters of our own race." I concluded, "John E. Brown College in its early years, like most educational institutions of the day, reflected the racial segregation of American society. Though non-white students would appear at the college by the 1940s, J.E.B.C. was intentionally white in its first two decades."[9] When *Head, Heart, and Hand* was published in 2003, its discussion of the institution's racialized past generally flew under the radar, and the book was widely read by students, alumni, board members, and other constituents. Such transparency, however, became problematic in subsequent years.

∞∞∞

While growing into my professional role at John Brown University, I was also becoming aware of the broader higher-education movement of which JBU was a part, including a growing network of like-minded institutions called the Council for Christian Colleges & Universities (CCCU). My first induction into the movement was a CCCU-led New Faculty Institute at Westmont College in Santa Barbara, California. In the summer of 1998, I traveled to Santa Barbara, a beautiful and exotic place by my Midwestern standards, for this three-day workshop led by Wheaton philosophy professor Arthur Holmes, who had written the popular book *The Idea of a Christian College* (1985); CCCU vice president Karen Longman; and Westmont provost Stan Gaede. (Strangely enough, I would eventually write a book on the Christian liberal arts in the tradition of Holmes, occupy Karen's role at the CCCU, and work at Stan's college.) The workshop itself focused on what was a fairly new concept to many of us Christian college professors at the time—how to integrate Christian faith with one's teaching. Throughout the decade, the CCCU developed a Through the Eyes of Faith book series (*Biology through the Eyes of Faith*, *History through the Eyes of Faith*, *Sociology through the Eyes of Faith*, etc.), and these books became standard reading on Christian college campuses.

While I don't remember much about the workshop other than walking the Wharf in Santa Barbara, faith integration was a topic that would assume growing importance in my own career. A couple of years later, JBU received a grant from the Teagle Foundation to conduct a series of summer faculty development workshops on faith integration for our own faculty. For a school like John Brown, with its vocational tradition and dispensationalist theological foundation, these were uncharted waters for most of us. I was on the faculty development committee at the time and so managed to worm my way onto the planning team for the workshop. Taking guidance from David Brisben and Ed Ericson, we compiled a volume consisting of articles by Reformed scholars such as George Marsden, Cornelius Plantinga (Alvin's brother), and Nicholas Wolterstorff, and basically figured out Christian faith integration—or at least argued over it—on our own. As one of the organizers of the workshop, it was a valuable learning experience in connecting my faith with my teaching, which many Christian professors across the nation were learning to do at the time.

ooooo

Like many evangelical colleges seeking greater academic respectability, John Brown University faced not only the challenge of a fundamentalist heritage but a physical location far from the cultural centers of power. In JBU's case, that location was northwest Arkansas, which despite the growing influence of Walmart, still displayed many traits of cultural populism. Typical of many rural college towns, Siloam Springs consisted of two communities—those associated with the university (and who were commonly transplants from other regions) and the locals. Churches, schools, school athletics, and the local Walmart provided something of a common ground, but generally the two communities operated independently from each other. For several years, Lonnie and I wondered why Siloam Springs was so quiet on Friday nights in autumn. Then some friends invited us to a high school football game, where it seemed the entire town was crammed into the home stands.

Like most JBU faculty, our primary friends were other community outsiders. These were people like David and Susan Brisben from South Carolina, Gary and Carrie Oliver from Denver, Wendy and Kai Tagami from Chicago, Steve and Jane Beers from Indiana, and the Stevensons—Billy from the Shankhill Road in Belfast,

Northern Ireland, and Mindi from a farm in Iowa. Because we lived just minutes apart, were far from family, and shared an interest in Christian higher education, our friendships grew unusually close, and many of them continue to this day.

Along with raising their academic stature, evangelical colleges of the 1990s like JBU were gingerly stepping away from fundamentalist moral restrictions, including alcohol consumption. Historically, JBU was a teetotaler institution. John Brown Sr. had been an adamant Prohibitionist, and it was largely through his efforts in the 1950s that Benton County had approved a law banning the sale of alcohol. As more theologically diverse faculty were hired in the 1990s, however, that began to change. By the time I joined JBU in 1997, the university's expectations concerning alcohol consumption had evolved to an ambiguous statement that the institution "vigorously discourages the use of alcohol, except for medicinal, culinary, or sacramental purposes." Since President Balzer astutely avoided overdefining that statement, it basically functioned as a Rorschach test open to a variety of interpretations, depending on the reader's perspective. Did "medicinal purposes" include a glass of bourbon as a sleeping aid? Perhaps. Did "culinary purposes" mean just a splash of red wine in the marinara sauce, or a hearty glass of Cabernet to accompany the meal? You decide.

Eventually, therefore, JBU's policy came to allow for the moderate use of alcohol simply because a significant segment of the JBU community came to interpret it that way. Other prominent Christian colleges and universities, including Wheaton and eventually even Moody, were also updating their policies at around this time, and each change made it easier for subsequent institutions to do the same without alienating their constituents. During my first semester at Cornerstone University in 2009, the institution changed its alcohol policy for faculty and staff. The president, fearing a backlash among conservative constituents, was pleasantly surprised to receive only one letter of complaint, perhaps because, by then, Grand Rapids had acquired the moniker of Beer City, USA. Evangelical colleges still have plenty of hot-button issues, but alcohol consumption is rarely one of them. Most Christian college professors nowadays can debate human origins over a pint of beer.

Another possible challenge of being an academician in a small town can be raising children. While rural Arkansas may have had some drawbacks, it provided significant benefits as well. In our case, one of those benefits was finding Northview, a three-acre homestead perched atop a small hill at the end of a 450-foot driveway and surrounded by forty acres of ranch land (at least until the subdivisions started creeping in). Thus, our children got to enjoy the best of both worlds—a house in the country that was located just three miles from town. In addition to fixing up the house, my obsessive habits led to the planting of hundreds of trees on the property, which provided valuable lessons in manual labor for the kids. During a drought, Ryan and Tyler had the privilege of hand-watering over three hundred seedlings as I towed a plastic tub filled with water up the long driveway. Each child had a section of the property to maintain with the John Deere riding mower. For Anna, we bungee-corded the seat down to prevent the kill switch from being activated as her six-year-old body bounced along the back pasture.

Our family life took a dramatic change, however, when I received a Fulbright Fellowship in 2004 to teach history at the University of Wurzburg in southern Germany. That March, we moved into a two-bedroom apartment in downtown Wurzburg. I taught two upper-level courses, the American Civil War and the History of the American West. While the smoke-filled student cafeteria took some getting used to, I had little difficulty adjusting to the German teaching schedule: both classes met for two hours every Thursday, which left plenty of time for the six Ostranders to tour Europe. Our arrival actually corresponded with the fiftieth anniversary of the Fulbright program in Berlin, so our first weekend in Germany included a train ride to Berlin and a stay at the Park Inn overlooking the city's famous Alexanderplatz. Other weeks were spent traveling by train and car to Austria, Switzerland, Italy, and France, with long unforgettable walks throughout the major cities of Europe.

One result of the Fulbright Fellowship was my introduction to the world of study abroad, an important aspect of higher education that I had not experienced as a student. By 2004, I had become an avid road biker, and my Trek road bike accompanied me to Germany. After a few months biking the back roads of northern Bavaria, I knew the nooks and crannies of the region better than most Germans. One of my rides led me through a quaint village along the Main River called Margetshöchheim, where I noticed a large old timber-framed farmhouse with a *Ferienhaus* (vacation house) sign posted outside. I inquired with the owner, a former BMW engineer from Munich, and learned that for a reasonable sum, the entire house could be rented out to a group of thirteen students plus two faculty for several weeks. Haus Zimmermann, as it was called, became base camp for a monthlong European Studies summer program that Lonnie and I led in partnership with other professors for the next five years. The Fulbright Fellowship not only exposed our children to the broader world but led to a new career pathway for me in international education that I would never have envisioned before my time in Germany.

∞∞∞

I returned from Germany in the fall of 2004 to a university that was making significant strides academically, and I assumed a role as academic dean in that process. The first six years at JBU were my induction into academic life as a faculty member. In my second six years, I learned academic life from the administrator's chair. The view can be quite different, and faculty have for good reason borrowed an old movie title, *Invasion of the Body Snatchers*, to describe what seems to happen when one of their peers moves into an administrative role. The body looks the same, but the words and actions seem strangely foreign. Perhaps a simpler way to describe the transformation is by that old adage, "where you stand depends on where you sit."

Actually, my first exposure to the inner workings of a university occurred a few years earlier when I became chair of the JBU Faculty Association. During the difficult one-year presidency following John Brown III's resignation, this body was created to provide a collective voice by which to communicate faculty concerns to the university's leadership. It met monthly to discuss faculty issues, and any concerns that emerged were communicated to the president and provost by way of the chair. Such a system obviously required a chair with a nuanced understanding of the university and an appreciation for the complex nature of institutions. Typical of academia, however, the leadership of the organization often fell to newbies who didn't have the good sense to decline the honor.

As a chair, my lack of awareness of how universities function was almost comical. At one point in my first year, the faculty compiled a list of concerns that they felt were not being adequately addressed by the administration. My proposed strategy was to write a letter to the board of trustees while cc'ing the president. When I mentioned this plan to the president during our monthly meeting, he gently steered me away from it and mentioned—correctly—that bypassing college leaders and directly contacting board members is a serious breach of institutional protocol. I did have good instincts, however, and believed that getting people to talk *to* each other rather than *about* each other might be more productive than separate gatherings. Thus, we instituted a monthly faculty-cabinet lunch in which the groups ate a meal together, then professors had the opportunity to ask questions directly to the president or a cabinet member. While such a practice inevitably created some awkward moments, seeing the ability of open, frank conversation to defuse tensions and correct misperceptions was a valuable lesson that I carried with me to future roles.

By my fifth year as a full-time professor, I had developed a desire to play a larger role in shaping the direction of the university. Thus, when my colleague Ed Ericson was promoted from dean of undergraduate studies to vice president for academic affairs, I applied for the dean position. I was selected as the new dean, but soon thereafter also received the Fulbright Fellowship. Thus, I enjoyed a warm-up fall semester as academic dean before heading off to Germany, then began the role in earnest upon my return in the fall of 2004. After six years on the faculty, I was now a full-time administrator and an official member of the Dark Side.

Books on academic leadership fill many shelves, but a lot of leadership is just learning by doing. One can read a manual on how to ride a bike, but ultimately one needs to get on the bike, start moving, and let the neurons and muscle fibers slowly figure it out—hopefully in a grassy field to cushion the inevitable falls. I'm grateful that John Brown University gave me the opportunity to learn the dean role, provided some guidance, and didn't overreact to the inevitable mistakes. One of my early lessons in academic leadership was that administrators are the embodiment of institutional decisions, whether or not they actually made the decisions themselves. For example, during my first year as dean, the university, after seeing nearly half of its students graduate "with honors," raised the GPA requirements for students to graduate cum laude, magna cum laude, and summa cum laude. I considered the change to be a victory for academic rigor and didn't think losing a few Latin words after one's name on the graduation program would be a big deal to students or parents. After several irate emails and phone calls from parents, however, I learned otherwise.

Ultimately, what attracted me to administration was the opportunity to apply the "recovering an evangelical mind" project that I had absorbed in graduate school on an institutional scale. Professors advance the life of the mind as teachers and scholars; administrators can shape entire institutions—or so I hoped. One area at JBU that seemed to offer significant potential to move the institutional needle academically was revamping the dreaded first-year seminar that was required for all freshman.

First-year seminars have become common in higher education because they fulfill important purposes for universities. For one, most independent, undergraduate-oriented institutions claim to be based on a liberal arts curriculum. But aside from a few "pure" liberal arts colleges, most of them must attract students by offering an array of majors such as business, education, and engineering. Then they engage in postsales marketing to persuade such students of the value of their liberal arts courses. Christian colleges face an additional challenge: since the 1990s, they have asserted that a Christian worldview impacts academic life, but they recruit evangelical students who have typically been conditioned to view "Christian" as something that occurs in chapel, not in the classroom.

Thus, first-year seminars seek to introduce students to the purpose and value of Christian higher education, help them transition to college life, and provide some skills needed to succeed academically. In other words, the first-year seminar typically is not just about education but retention—keeping new students from struggling during their first semester, going home, and taking their tuition dollars with them. Such courses often become a catch basin for everything from Christian worldview to study skills to Enneagram tests to getting along with a roommate. Students emerge dazed and eager to get to General Chemistry class, where at least the content of the course is tangible.

JBU's version of the first-year seminar was Foundations of Christian Scholarship (FCS), which badly needed revision. The content was about as engaging as the title, and since most professors avoided teaching it, sections were taught by anyone from student development staff to coaches. In course evaluations, students consistently rated FCS at the bottom along with Technology and Society (otherwise known as Tech and Suck). Here was a fun project to take on, both because I was an enthusiastic adult convert to the Christian liberal arts and faith integration, and because it was unlikely I could make the class more unpopular than it already was. Thus, we assembled a task force of professors and staff members, most of whom were relative newcomers to JBU like myself, and set to work on reenvisioning the course.

The result one year later was the Gateway Seminar in Christian Scholarship. The course was consolidated into two basic purposes: to help students understand the purpose and value of a Christian liberal arts education, and to provide some basic approaches to integrating faith and learning. Classes met Monday and Wednesday, and we off-loaded the other elements of "College Life 101" onto weekly Friday sessions, of which students had to attend a certain number. Steve Beers, vice president for student development, was a close friend and biking partner, and our hundreds of hours on the road together provided ample opportunity to discuss ways that academics and student life could collaborate in the course.

Gateway Seminar sought to teach Christian higher education indirectly: professors taught whatever topic they were most interested in, but they were required to use the topic to demonstrate the value of the liberal arts and the difference that a Christian approach to learning makes. Topics ranged from Harry Potter to the Chronicles of Narnia, and from Islamic art to Native American literature. Also, the class met two hours a week, but it counted as three hours of teaching load for professors, which meant that I was able to recruit the university's best professors to teach sections of the course. The revised content and format, combined with skilled teachers, made a significant improvement. While not perfect, it did successfully induct students into the Christian liberal arts and provided a common foundation that other professors could build upon throughout their students' academic journeys.

For me personally, Gateway Seminar also extended my writing career in an unexpected new direction. For a common text, we compiled a course pack of various writings by Christian scholars, the success of which was spotty at best. Meanwhile, after writing *Head, Heart, and Hand*, I had come to realize that my scholarly niche was not in becoming another George Marsden but rather in taking the ideas of important scholars and putting them on a lower shelf where they could be accessed by students and general readers. Thus, I began filling in the gaps in the course pack with my own writings and replacing the texts that did not seem to resonate with students. Eventually, realizing that I had most of a book written myself, I reached out to a colleague with connections at Abilene Christian University Press. The result was a book, *Why College Matters to God: An Introduction to Christian Learning* (2009), that has been adopted by a variety of Christian colleges and universities over the past several years. Christian academia needs first-rate thinkers advancing a scholarly voice in the academy, but it also needs translators and popularizers who can communicate important ideas to a general audience, and fortunately I was able to find a niche in the latter group.

ooooo

After several years as a dean, I had settled into a comfortable groove at JBU. Lonnie and I had a lovely house, four children who were adept at yard work, good jobs at a stable institution, and a network of close friendships. Nevertheless, a sense of restlessness was growing in me. Like many administrators, my "achiever" personality feeds on accomplishing things, whether biking up a summit, painting a house, or creating a new academic program. During my time at JBU, my colleagues and I had accomplished much: the new Gateway Seminar was established; we overhauled the core curriculum; global education had expanded significantly; and probably most importantly, we had taken advantage of the buyers' market in academia to recruit a host of bright young Christian professors. The next phase of my work as a dean, it seemed, would be primarily continuing the momentum of what had been established, but "maintenance" was not a concept that fired my imagination. Moreover, after several runner-up placements in the intramural basketball A-league, my team finally won the championship, helped in part by the reluctance of student referees to call fouls on the dean. Thus, despite our comfortable situation in Siloam Springs—or perhaps because of it—I was open to moving elsewhere.

A few opportunities had presented themselves, but none of them seemed right. Then in the fall of 2008, I received a phone call from Joseph Stowell at Cornerstone University in Grand Rapids, Michigan. Joe had become president at Moody Bible Institute in 1987, soon after I graduated. My father served with him for several years as assistant to the president, so I knew of Joe and thought highly of him. He retired from Moody in 2002, spent a few years preaching and writing, then took the helm at Cornerstone in spring 2008. The following fall, Cornerstone launched a provost search, and Joe inquired as to whether I was interested in the role. I didn't know if I was, but I was intrigued enough to apply. During my student days at Michigan, Ann Arborites referred to Grand Rapids as Bland Rapids, but apparently the city had improved over the past two decades. The search process eventually led to a mid-February visit by Lonnie and me, with the city buried in the customary blanket of lake-effect snow. Such weather may have been daunting to the other finalist, who hailed from Southern California, but to me it felt like being home again.

A few weeks later, when the offer came from Cornerstone, we were faced with a significant life decision once again. Unlike Phoenix twelve years earlier, there was no difficult situation encouraging us to look elsewhere. Nevertheless, professionally and spiritually, it seemed that I had plateaued at John Brown and was ready for something else. A provost position, with a host of new challenges to meet and projects to accomplish, seemed like the right move after six years as dean. Of course, our children were an important consideration, but if we were ever going to move away from Arkansas during their school years, 2009 seemed to be the right time. Ryan had graduated from high school and was on his way to Messiah University in Pennsylvania; Rachel was beginning high school in the fall; and Anna was moving from elementary school to junior high. Tyler was entering his senior year of high school but was nonetheless amenable to a move. Whether such inner promptings and external indicators are God's way of guiding us in particular directions, or whether as Christians we simply make choices and later perceive them as God's inevitable leading, is one of those mysterious questions that I continue to ponder. Whatever the case, after much prayer and deliberation, we made the decision to move to Cornerstone and prepared to say good-bye to our friends in Siloam Springs.

ooooo

The 1990s and early years of the new century were flush times for Christian higher education. Most institutions saw their enrollments and budgets expand. The demographic, enrollment, and financial challenges that have afflicted private colleges and universities since the 2008 recession had not yet arrived. Christian colleges were heeding Mark Noll and seeking to overcome evangelicalism's historic anti-intellectualism, and many were succeeding quite well at it. I'm grateful that I could use my experience at Moody, Michigan, and Notre Dame to help one such institution make significant strides. Subsequent events would suggest that my leaving was well timed, and that JBU didn't need my help to continue its academic and institutional progress.

That progress was assured when Chip Pollard succeeded Lee Balzer as president of JBU in 2004. In many ways, Chip had the ideal pedigree for a Christian college president. The son of a business executive, he boasted an academic résumé that included a BA from Wheaton College, a master's degree from Oxford University, a JD from Harvard, and a PhD in English from the University of Virginia. When JBU launched its presidential search in the spring of 2004, Chip was serving as an assistant professor of English at Calvin College and was on no one's presidential search list. Ed Ericson's father at Calvin, however, tipped us off, and since I was traveling to West Michigan, I met with Chip for a long conversation about Christian higher education and John Brown University. After our talk, I wrote to the search committee nominating Chip for president. The search committee concurred, and a few months later he was named JBU's new president.

Under Chip's leadership, John Brown University has continued to develop into a first-rate institution. Today JBU enrolls approximately 1,400 full-time undergraduate students and another 500 in master's and degree-completion programs. For the past few years, it has been able to tout itself as the highest-ranked regional university in Arkansas in the *U.S. News and World Report* college rankings. Moreover, in the past decade, JBU has played a significant role in shaping the identity and direction of the Council for Christian Colleges & Universities. Chip served as chair of the board of the CCCU from 2013 to 2018, and all of JBU's cabinet members have served in leadership roles among their respective peer organizations. In the broader world of US higher education, John Brown University might be fairly obscure, but within evangelicalism, the school is well known and respected.

Nevertheless, like many Christian colleges, JBU exists within a conservative subculture on which it depends for students and financial support, and in such an environment, overcoming the "scandal" of evangelical populism and anti-intellectualism remains a continuous challenge. That fact was apparent to me during my last semester at the university. Some conservative alumni, concerned that students were not being adequately instructed in young-earth creationism, agitated for a lecture series on creation and evolution so that they could address this deficiency. As academic dean, I became responsible for the project. In addition to having the alums present their views, I invited a physicist from Calvin College named Deborah Haarsma to speak on the topic. Dr. Haarsma, who would go on to lead the Christian scientific organization BioLogos, gave an eloquent defense of theistic evolution, which angered the alums, some board members, and a former Bible professor. I subsequently moved to Grand Rapids, leaving Chip to manage the fallout for the next two years.

Sadly, in recent years, my own relationship to JBU has become a casualty of the increasing polarization of American evangelicalism. Though my book on JBU history had attempted to place John Brown Sr.'s racial views in historical context, the portrait of the founder irked some supporters of the university. The situation was exacerbated in recent years by a group of younger, more socially progressive alumni who stirred up controversy by portraying JBU as a historically racist institution, and they cited some passages from my book in support. As a result, some conservative constituents came to criticize not only my book on JBU history but also the Gateway Seminar and the university's growing emphasis on the liberal arts. *Head, Heart, and Hand* disappeared from JBU a few years before the school's 100th anniversary celebration in 2019, replaced by a book on the history of the university compiled by the founder's grandson. Despite being the former institutional historian, I was not invited to participate in the anniversary celebration.

Such are the complications that accompany being a Christian university in a small town in a red state in the Bible Belt. For our family, while the larger urban setting of Grand Rapids wasn't a deciding factor in our decision to leave, we did welcome a move to such a setting. Ironically for a beer geek like me, soon after our departure, Benton County dropped its dry ordinance, and a charming little brewery opened in downtown Siloam Springs, complete with an outdoor patio and cornhole pitch. The opening of such an establishment wouldn't have kept me in Siloam Springs, but it would have made the decision to leave even more difficult. At any rate, in the summer of 2009, we said good-bye to friends, sold our beloved Northview home to the incoming campus pastor, and drove our Honda Odyssey to Grand Rapids. We gladly turned over the customary wrestling of the battle-tested Kawai to the moving van professionals.

FIVE

Academic Leadership

Aᴙᴙɪᴠɪɴɢ ɪɴ Gᴙᴀɴᴅ Rᴀᴘɪᴅs in the summer of 2009, Lonnie and I settled into the tree-shaded community of East Grand Rapids, whose walkable neighborhoods reminded us of our time in Germany. Gerald Ford's boyhood home sat several blocks down from our white corner house at 2466 Lake Drive—the house with the wraparound porch, as it was known in the neighborhood. Our kids were quick to pick up on the social contrast from Arkansas. Rachel, beginning her freshman year of high school, mowed the front lawn covered by her hoodie, not because of the colder weather but because not using a professional lawn service was a rarity in our community. Also, from the raised eyebrows of some people at Cornerstone, I learned that "East" was known as something of a liberal Democrat enclave in a Republican city; it certainly led the city in the percentage of Obama bumper stickers. In August, Ryan headed off to Messiah College in Pennsylvania, the other kids began school in East, Lonnie joined the Grand Rapids Ballet as staff pianist, and I settled into my new job as provost.

∞∞∞

Cornerstone University was founded in 1941 as the Baptist Bible Institute of Grand Rapids. Like John Brown University, it was a product of Protestant fundamentalist institution-building. In the 1920s, Northern Baptists splintered into several subgroups. One of them was the General Association of Regular Baptists, or GARB for short. Emphasizing strict legalism and doctrinal conservatism, GARBs established churches and colleges across the Northeast and Upper Midwest. Three of the most prominent were Cedarville College in Ohio, Baptist Bible College in Pennsylvania, and Grand Rapids Baptist. The latter ended its official affiliation with the GARB denomination in 1993, absorbed another college, the Grand Rapids School of Bible and Music, and became Cornerstone University in 1999. Its ties to local conservative churches in the Midwest, however, remained strong.

For me, coming to Cornerstone represented the closing of a circle in some ways: When I was born in Fort Wayne, Indiana, my father served as minister of music at Immanuel Baptist Church, a prominent GARB institution. As a child, I had painful memories of leaving home for Sunday evening church just as the opening scene of the *Wonderful World of Disney* was coming on the TV, with Tinkerbell waving her magic wand and flitting around the screen. Later, when I played basketball at Moody Bible Institute, each winter we would drive the vans to Grand Rapids to play Grand Rapids Baptist, Grand Rapids School of Bible and Music, and Grace Bible College.

Christian higher education in the United States is like a Seurat painting: from a distance, the dots blend together; but the closer one stands, the more the dots separate themselves into different colors and shapes. For example, John Brown University and Cornerstone resemble each other in terms of size—about two thousand students—and programs. However, whereas JBU represents a relatively well-resourced institution in a growing region of the United States, Cornerstone is one of countless universities scattered across America's northern tier and competing for students in a shrinking market. Cornerstone University began in the basement of Wealthy Street Baptist Church, which is ironic since the school historically has been anything but affluent. In fact, there are two important things to know about West Michigan. First, it is the bastion of Dutch Christian Reformed culture in America. Entrepreneurs such as Rich DeVos and Jay Van Andel (founders of Amway), Edgar

Prince, J. C. Huizenga, and Herman Miller have built profitable corporations that fund a vast number of civic organizations and nonprofits in the area. The second thing to know is that when it comes to Christian higher education, the two Reformed institutions, Calvin University and Hope College, sit at the front of the line. Others compete for the crumbs that fall from the Reformed philanthropic table. And in the middle of the 2008 recession, Cornerstone, like many private colleges and universities, needed more than just crumbs.

Fortunately for Cornerstone, its new president was well suited for such challenges. Tall, extroverted, and invariably optimistic, Joe Stowell dominated any room that he entered. He could joke privately about the sheriff coming to padlock the university's doors, then convene an all-campus meeting and assure faculty and staff that everything would be okay. Some leaders who "work a room" spark cynicism, especially among academics, but Joe's genuine love of people and the job of president was just woven into his personality. The son of a prominent GARB minister and a Cedarville University graduate, Joe had impeccable conservative credentials, but he lacked the fundamentalist nature of his predecessor at Cornerstone, whose best-known publication was a book condemning gambling. Despite his public stature, Joe had a humble streak and an ability to laugh at himself. An avid supporter of Cornerstone athletics, once he was standing along the sidelines of a men's soccer match when the ball rolled out of bounds past him. As he bounded to chase the ball, he stumbled, tore his left hamstring, and spent the next month on crutches. A video chronicling the event preceded his next chapel address.

Joe's cheerful disposition enabled him to persist at the difficult task of fund-raising for a non-Reformed institution in West Michigan, which sometimes required creative methods. A few years into my time there, a wealthy donor had a grandson coming to Cornerstone who wanted to play baseball. Cornerstone didn't have a baseball team or a facility, but it did need another residence hall. The solution was probably America's only combined baseball field and dormitory, with the residence hall wrapping around the stands and the field, providing students with luxury indoor seats for Cornerstone baseball games. Some professors were scandalized, but later Joe's adaptability paid off when the same donor gave millions toward a badly needed chapel building.

The chapel was also the beneficiary of one of Joe's greatest fundraising successes. Roberta Green Ahmanson is a noted evangelical author and philanthropist who began her academic career at Cornerstone in the late 1960s. Repelled by the legalism of the college at the time, she transferred to Calvin, later married the wealthy investor Howard Ahmanson, and devoted her career to philanthropy, and in particular to strengthening evangelical Christianity's involvement in the arts. A 2011 *Christianity Today* article about Roberta began by recounting her student days at Cornerstone, after which Joe wrote her a letter but received no response. A year later, Joe and I were attending a conference at Biola University and were seated at a round table eating lunch with several other guests. Sitting across from us was a vivacious middle-aged woman sporting bold red spectacles. She looked across the table at Joe and exclaimed, "I'm Roberta Ahmanson and I went to your school." A long conversation ensued, which led to a friendship between Roberta and Joe. Learning of Cornerstone's plans for a new chapel, Roberta concluded that the building needed beautiful stained glass windows. She then paid for Peter Brandes, a noted artist from Denmark, to spend six months in Grand Rapids creating four twenty-five-foot-high stained glass windows, which have become the campus's signature works of art.

Joe, the former GARB pastor, and I, a former professor, worked well together, and our differences complemented each other. Joe was the extroverted public figure; I was the quiet, "get things done" academician. When I was informed that during another provost candidate's interview with the cabinet, his wife sat in a corner reading a book, I joked that what got me the job was that during my interview, Lonnie talked with the cabinet while I sat in a corner reading a book. Joe was patient as I learned the ropes of a new role that I hadn't served in before. My most immediate task as provost was obvious: the university faced a significant budget deficit that required, among other things, the elimination of several faculty positions. The situation was further complicated by strained relations between faculty and administration. Before his departure, the previous president had persuaded the board of trustees to vote to abolish tenure for professors hired from that point on. Needless to say, the decision, made without faculty consultation, did not sit well with professors.

The university had conducted a program prioritization process before I arrived, but it had not taken action on the recommendations. As the new provost, I reviewed the report and identified the professors whose positions needed to be eliminated at the end of the academic year. I had never fired someone before and, as one should, experienced significant anxiety over the prospect. But I summoned my courage, called each person to my office, along with the accompanying division chair, and gave them the news as succinctly and empathetically as possible. In one memorable meeting, the division chair broke down in tears and was comforted by the person being terminated. We then informed the university community which positions were being eliminated, and we scheduled going-away receptions for those who wanted them. Attending those receptions was uncomfortable for me as the one who had done the terminating, but I owed those individuals the respect to show up and endure the potential awkwardness. Moreover, publicly honoring those who were being let go helped to rebuild a healthy culture of trust and transparency among the faculty and administration.

ooooo

Aside from the budget cuts, my early years as provost at Cornerstone were generally enjoyable and fulfilling. My assistant, Liz Wheeler, informed me that I was the fifth provost whom she had worked for in the past ten years. The frequent turnover in leadership meant that there were a lot of things that needed to be put in order. As an inveterate "fixer-upper," helping to strengthen an institution was fun and rewarding work. For example, we launched a task force to restore a system of faculty tenure that included clear standards and procedures for promotion and post-tenure review. The board approved the task force's proposal, which helped to improve relations on that front.

Addressing the proliferation of programs and courses, we launched a curriculum-streamlining initiative that set clear limits on the size of majors and minors. We held a "Committee Summit" to reduce the number of committees and set a clear mandate for each committee. Regarding the university's educational objectives, we launched an initiative to reduce the university's fifty-two (yes, fifty-two) student learning outcomes to six main goals, each with six supporting objectives. Because evaluations for academic administrators had generally dissipated, we created evaluations for deans, division chairs, and the provost, which gave the faculty the same opportunity to provide confidential feedback about their superiors that their students were given for them.

As an energetic new provost, sometimes my "uber-implementer" personality, as one professor called it, created problems for me. During my first year, the Bible Division was conducting searches to fill two faculty vacancies, and while the first slot was filled relatively easily, different perspectives within the division prevented agreement on which finalists should be invited to campus to interview for the second slot. Rather than slowing down and working through the differences in perspectives, my driven, task-oriented nature led me to continue pushing to bring candidates to campus and try to close the deal before summer. Fortunately, a veteran member of the department pointed out to me that my obsession with finishing the search was undermining my relationship with the division. We halted the search, hired a temporary person for the following academic year, and I embarked on a personal apology tour of the division.

Also, in my second year, I had what seemed to me a great idea of expanding the customary fall faculty workshop into an overnight retreat at a nearby conference center on Lake Michigan. As planning for the event progressed, Pete Muir, the Communications Division chair and an Australian with a penchant for frank conversation, informed me that most professors preferred to prep their fall course syllabi rather than endure a forced morale-building overnight retreat. I managed to do a retreat myself, and sent out an email canceling the event and attempting to salvage my reputation with a sarcastic email about hosting a slumber party at my house instead. Sometimes my sarcasm in communications could go sideways as well. For instance, Cornerstone had a summer reading program in which a faculty committee selected a book for professors to read over the summer and discuss at the fall faculty workshop. On one April Fool's Day, I emailed the faculty informing them that the committee had selected my book, *Why College Matters to God*, as the faculty summer reading text. I thought that my email had the perfect blend of realism and absurdity, but then had second thoughts when two professors contacted me to ask where to send their checks for the book.

ooooo

Beyond particular projects, Cornerstone's rocky history of faculty/ administration relations meant that investing in relationships with faculty was a crucial, though time-consuming, part of the job in restoring a culture of trust. In some ways, my introverted personality created challenges as a provost. At all-faculty and staff gatherings, I sometimes shied away from giving detailed, enthusiastic updates on academic affairs, which left the faculty with the impression that the university cared more about athletics and student development than academics. In other ways, however, taking Susan Cain's advice in *Quiet: The Power of Introverts in a World That Can't Stop Talking* (2013), I learned to leverage my introverted nature to my advantage as a leader. While Joe thrived in public gatherings, I did my best work in more personal settings, visiting professors in their offices to hear their advice; spending hours in the dining commons eating lunch with professors, coaches, and staff; and hosting professors and spouses in our home for dinner. On a college campus, many of the most important faculty conversations occur spontaneously in the hallways, so I developed a habit after lunch of making a circuit of the campus and dropping in on as many faculty offices as possible.

Also, since writing came more naturally to me than speaking, I also learned to maximize the role of the pen as an academic leader.

Even at small universities such as Cornerstone, communication across the organization can be difficult, and professors are adept at filling in information vacuums with theories and speculations. Thus, I developed a routine of sending out a "provost's update" email every Friday afternoon, which summarized developments at the university while also inserting my own perspective on the issues and reflections on higher education in general.

ooooo

Despite some accomplishments and a general improvement in faculty morale, the basic underlying reality at Cornerstone, like that of many private colleges and universities that I have worked with since, was a scarcity of resources. Cornerstone's endowment when I arrived was around $6 million (John Brown's, by contrast, was over $100 million). That, combined with highly discounted tuition in order to recruit students, meant that budgets were typically stretched to the limit, and often it felt like we were making do with duct tape and chewing gum. It wasn't quite the offices in house trailers that I encountered at Grand Canyon, but relative scarcity tended to affect most things at Cornerstone, from faculty salaries to science facilities to athletic fields.

Like many of its peers in the 1990s, Cornerstone had developed online, graduate, and adult degree completion programs to generate additional revenue. But nontraditional education was a competitive market as well, and other regional Christian universities such as Spring Arbor and Indiana Wesleyan splashed their logos on billboards around West Michigan. For some of our board members, Liberty University, its campus swimming in cash from vast online enrollments, seemed like the model to emulate. Joe and I became accustomed to the question at board meetings, "Liberty's making millions from online; why aren't we doing that?" They seemed to have a hard time accepting the fact that the online education gravy train had left the station years earlier, and latecomer institutions simply did their best to jump onto the rear cars. Moreover, the academic decisions that some online institutions made to create a profitable business model were not ones that we would have been comfortable with at Cornerstone.

One memorable artifact of life on a tight budget was the Faculty Office Building, the brainchild of my colleague, Executive Vice President Marc Fowler. Before I arrived at Cornerstone, due to declining enrollments, a dormitory called Quincer Hall had been converted to faculty offices. Fortunately, increasing enrollments under Joe Stowell's presidency required that we use Quincer again for students, which raised the question of where to put the faculty. Marc learned of two modular buildings near Detroit that had belonged to General Motors and that were now available for a low price. We poured a cement slab next to the Teacher Education Building and had a truck haul the modulars across the state. Builders stitched the two buildings together, and once they put a sloped roof over the top, from a distance one could hardly detect the building's prefab nature. As the building settled, however, several office doors failed to close fully. Also, neglecting to take into account the thin walls and false floor, we put a classroom in the middle of the building. Students and faculty walking down the hallways sounded like Frankenstein's monster as their thudding footsteps echoed through the walls and floor into the classroom. Some of the faculty inhabitants named the building "Fowler's Folly," though to Marc's credit, the building has endured the Michigan winters rather well and continues to fill an important need on campus.

While finances remained a challenge, one area that we did find resources for was technology. In the first decades of the 2000s, many experts were predicting an impending "tsunami" of digital education that would sweep away traditional education as we knew it. As luck would have it, Cornerstone's new campus technology director was a "Mac" guy who wanted to move the university to Apple devices right when Apple as a company was investing heavily in education. As a result, several of us flew to Cupertino, California, where, like the Golden Ticket winners in *Charlie and the Chocolate Factory*, we were treated to a daylong feast of the latest educational technology and gadgets at Apple's world headquarters.

While Cornerstone subsequently did make some progress in digital learning, I tended to identify with my traditionalist colleagues in the Humanities Division such as philosophy professor

Matt Bonzo, a Wendell Berry disciple who ran a small farm north of the city, and Michael Stevens, who was thoroughly and charmingly inept with technology. Cornerstone developed some online programs and, like most other institutions, began requiring professors to post their syllabi on this new "learning management system" thing called Blackboard, but I provided administrative cover for professors who preferred to remain old-school in their teaching and ban laptops from their classrooms. Also, after my visit to Cupertino, I penned an article for *Books and Culture* on the value of traditional low-tech education, "Learning to Surf: A Christian College Provost Encounters the Digital Revolution," that has remained one of my favorite writings.

⚬⚬⚬⚬⚬

Between the heavy workload, chronically tight budgets, and the occasional termination of employees, the role of the chief academic officer in Christian higher education is a difficult one. Nationwide, in fact, the average tenure for a provost is only about five years. The real reason for the short life span, however, isn't the finances or the firings. It's that the provost serves as the fulcrum point between the university's academic and nonacademic constituencies. One can envision a university as a manual transmission in a car, with various groups—faculty, students, staff, alumni, president, board—as the gears. The provost is the clutch, whose job is to manage the inevitable friction generated by the shifting of the gears. Thus, like a clutch, it's virtually inherent in the provost position to be worn down and eventually replaced. In good conditions—small intervals between gears, a careful driver—the provost can last for a long time, and some do. But when you have misaligned gears, or a sixteen-year-old driver intent on squealing the tires at every traffic light, the clutch can wear down pretty fast.

There's an old quip that gets trotted out at provost conferences: "The job of the president is to speak in public, the job of the faculty is to think, and the job of the provost to keep the president from thinking and keep the faculty from speaking in public." Like many jokes, it rests on an exaggeration of reality. Many professors are gifted public speakers, but in general they tend to be experts in narrow fields and independently minded. Sometimes they don't consider their institution's broader constituency when they speak or blog on controversial subjects. Presidents are smart, of course, but they're also very busy and rarely have time to delve deeply into academic issues that occupy the time of the faculty, or they need to simplify complex issues for public consumption. Moreover, they report to board members who are often wealthy alums from the corporate world or pastors with rigid theological perspectives.

In the highly competitive market of private, faith-based higher education, controversy between constituents that goes public can be disastrous. When I was at John Brown University, a professor at a Christian college in the Midwest attracted attention for espousing what he called "open theism," or the notion that God doesn't know the future. Whether such an idea was heretical or not, the bottom line for the college was that for a few years, many youth pastors who used to recommend it to their students stopped doing so, and enrollment dipped, which resulted in budget cuts and lost jobs. In other words, academic freedom sounds great for the big players such as the University of Michigan, but if it means that you're down fifty new students in the fall, everyone feels the pinch. And when that happens, people tend to look to the provost and exclaim, "How did you let this happen?" The provost, therefore, sometimes feels like the host of a Thanksgiving dinner for a family made up of Sanders and Trump supporters. If you keep the conversation centered on football, things go fine, but if it veers to politics, you might end up with cold turkey and uneaten pumpkin pie.

Over the past two decades, two of the biggest potential dinner-spoilers in Christian higher education have been human origins and human sexuality, and they certainly impacted my life as a provost at Cornerstone. Regarding origins, Cornerstone's Science Division was a bastion of young-earth creationism, thanks to a longtime division chair who only hired professors who espoused that position. My first year at Cornerstone, the *Grand Rapids Press* carried a front-page story about how the various colleges in the region handled the teaching of evolution. It cited a Calvin science professor in support of evolution, and then went on to describe Cornerstone as vigorously opposed to evolution. I knew, however, that there were Cornerstone professors in the Bible Division who, if asked, would have espoused theistic evolution. At my first board meeting, therefore, when a board member gave an impassioned defense of young-earth creationism, it was clear that this was an issue ripe for controversy at Cornerstone.

While the conversation about origins at the board level was out of my hands, I could at least try to break down barriers between the Science and Bible Divisions, which were hardly on speaking terms regarding the subject. Fortunately, a new organization had just been formed in Grand Rapids called the Colossian Forum, whose goal was not to resolve disagreements among Christians, but rather to help them see the disagreements themselves as opportunities to practice Christian virtues of civility and hospitality. The organization's founder, Michael Gulker, was looking for some initial organizations that would try out his method, and he had enlisted a philosopher from Calvin College, James K. A. Smith, to help him. I invited Michael and James to lead a one-day, off-campus, closed-door retreat for the Science and Bible Divisions.

The following year, my former professor at Moody, John Walton, was taking a sabbatical from his teaching post at Wheaton College to embark on a speaking tour on Genesis and origins. John had written *The Lost World of Genesis One: Ancient Cosmology and the Origins Debate* (2009) and had become known as someone who could gently persuade fellow evangelicals to read the early chapters of Genesis without imposing modern scientific categories on the text. We invited John to Cornerstone, where he gave an evening lecture, made some classroom visits, and hosted an interactive lunch session with the faculty. Legitimate disagreements over origins persisted, as they do in evangelicalism as a whole, but I counted it a success that members of the Science Department at least came to accept the notion that theistic evolutionists could be legitimate Christians.

The origins issue at Cornerstone was complicated by the fact that we were also embarking on a revision of the university's foundational doctrinal statement, the Cornerstone Confession. As provost, I was asked to cochair a task force to review the document and suggest changes. In general, the revisions were in the direction of creating a broader statement and removing Cornerstone's Baptist vestiges, but regarding creation, the movement was more complicated. Cornerstone's previous doctrinal statement, like that of many evangelical institutions, simply stated, "God created Adam and Eve . . ." As controversy swirled among evangelicals over creation and evolution, however, it was unclear whether such a minimal statement would be adequate for some of the conservative constituents that such colleges relied on. The young-earth populist Ken Ham, for example, not only built the Creation Museum in Kentucky to promote young-earth creationist views but published a book, *Already Compromised* (2011), that identified a small number of "safe" Christian colleges that espoused a literalist interpretation of Genesis.

One of our institutional models at Cornerstone, Wheaton College, had a contentious history with the subject of evolution. Outside observers of Christian higher education typically view Wheaton as emblematic of the movement in general. The reality, however, is that Wheaton tends toward the more conservative end of the Christian college spectrum. Concerning human origins, Wheaton has historically sought to define the issue more narrowly, whereas other leading evangelical colleges such as Gordon, Point Loma, and Westmont affirm creation but leave the question of means undefined. Under Duane Litfin's presidency, the board revised Wheaton's doctrinal statement to include the line "God directly created Adam and Eve, the historical parents of the entire human race"—language that seemed to rule out any possibility of human evolution.

In our Cornerstone Confession task force, that little adverb, "directly," occupied much of our conversation. Eventually, as at Wheaton, it found its way into the confession, but the result was that we had to thread the linguistic needle: Outsiders who read the document might assume that "directly" ruled out any form of human evolution. Cornerstone faculty and staff, however, might interpret "directly" to refer to Adam and Eve's spiritual natures, not necessarily their physical bodies. Concerning the latter, some evolutionary process might have been involved. Thus, we managed the potential friction between the various gears of the institution, but whenever conversations with board members drifted toward Genesis and human origins, I felt an instinctive urge to change the subject to sports or the weather.

∞∞∞

In more recent years, debates over marriage and human sexuality have overshadowed the origins controversy. As homosexuality became more accepted in mainstream culture, Christian colleges increasingly came to be seen as out of step. Moreover, many schools, rooted in traditional interpretations of Scripture, simply assumed that homosexual activity was off-limits for Christians but hadn't actually encoded such views in institutional documents. The situation, therefore, was ripe for controversy and potential lawsuits.

In 1998, Mel White, a former speechwriter for Jerry Falwell and Billy Graham who had come out as a gay man, founded Soulforce, an organization dedicated to combating discrimination against homosexual, queer, and transgender individuals. In 2006, the organization launched Equality Rides, in which members toured the country by bus, visiting Christian colleges and calling for an end to antigay policies at the institutions. When I was at John Brown University, we were too far off the cultural grid to merit a visit, but Grand Rapids was not. In 2007, a year before Joe Stowell's arrival, Soulforce visited Calvin and Cornerstone. Calvin, led by vice president of student development Shirley Hoogstra, took a hospitable posture and hosted on-campus conversations with the riders. Cornerstone took a harder line, banning the riders from campus (although some professors took it upon themselves to take lunch to the protesters off-campus). When two riders came onto campus anyway, they were arrested for trespassing. Needless to say, the coverage in the local press was hardly a public relations triumph for Cornerstone.

Joe Stowell was a traditionalist when it came to the issue of homosexuality, but he was astute at avoiding political controversy. During his presidency at Moody, for example, he drew the wrath of the popular conservative author James Dobson when Moody Radio stopped broadcasting Dobson's *Focus on the Family* daily show because it became too political. We also recognized that, like other Christian colleges, Cornerstone ran the risk of a lawsuit if it applied discriminatory hiring policies regarding homosexual behavior if it had no official document stating an institutional stance. The challenge for Cornerstone was to articulate an orthodox position on marriage and sexuality without being depicted by the *Grand Rapids Press* as bigots or ending up in the crosshairs of a gay rights organization.

Since the revision of the Cornerstone Confession was already in process, the new version included language supporting a traditional view of marriage. In addition, in the spring of 2013, Joe appointed me to lead a task force to draft a university statement on human sexuality that would balance a traditional biblical position with a nuanced awareness of the complexity of the issues and the need to support all members of the community. The resulting statement, I thought, was a good one, and included language such as "we are committed to treating all members of the community, whether heterosexual or homosexual, with love and respect and nurturing them as brothers and sisters in Christ." The document circulated throughout the university in fall 2013 and, after several revisions, was approved by the board in February 2014.

Two months later, my relationship to the issue took an unexpected turn. Our second son, Tyler, a talented artist, attended Gordon College, which had one of the best art departments among Christian colleges. In April, I was attending a Personnel Committee meeting with other cabinet members and began discreetly scrolling through emails on my phone. I noticed an email from Tyler to Lonnie and me and immediately opened it. Tyler bravely informed us that he was gay, and that he didn't want to end his four years at Gordon without coming out and finally being authentic to who he was. It was one of those moments as a parent when you know your next action could have lasting implications, and fortunately my innate sarcasm came to my aid. "Well, you certainly know how to liven up a boring Personnel Committee meeting," I thumbed back to him.

So what does a provost at an evangelical Christian university do when his son comes out? My first priority, of course, was to be a loving father and maintain a good relationship with my son. Lonnie and I talked on the phone with Tyler, discussing how he might best communicate to others, while also appropriately spreading the news ourselves. A few days later, I informed Joe. He received the news well, and like me, learned to live with the complexities. After all, I certainly wasn't the first Christian college professional to have a gay family member. Tyler's sexual orientation, and my support for him, was not something that I announced to the Cornerstone community, but it was also something I didn't shy away from if the subject came up. Soon thereafter, a faculty candidate came to campus for an interview. In the course of our conversation, he mentioned that he had an adult lesbian daughter, and I assured him that it wouldn't affect his prospects (he was subsequently hired).

Being a Christian higher-education professional with a gay son turned out to be a benefit to me, especially when I moved to a new role at the Council for Christian Colleges & Universities working with over one hundred institutions. I could still support the right of colleges to abide by traditional biblical values—that's what cultural pluralism is all about, after all—but I could also better identify with gay students on our campuses and the difficult and alienating experiences that they often encounter. In some ways, I learned to live in microcosm the life of a Christian college—to affirm traditional values but also to maintain that relationship supersedes theology. If doing so is paradoxical, as a father I'll take paradox over consistency.

Tyler graduated from Gordon and, tired of the dreary gray winters of New England and West Michigan, moved to California, where he eventually completed a second degree (in biology) at another Christian college, Point Loma Nazarene University. As an adult, he has made his own decisions in life and is in a committed relationship. A couple of years ago, on a business trip to San Diego, I met him for dinner and told him that I was proud of the man he had become. While his experience at Christian institutions as a gay man was decidedly mixed, I'm pleased that he has degrees from not one but two Christian colleges.

ooooo

Four years into my time at Cornerstone as the uber-implementer, the sense of restlessness and need for new challenges began to emerge. During my closing lunch at JBU with Chip Pollard, he had remarked, "The higher you rise in an organization, the more important alignment with the institution becomes." While my relationship with Joe and the rest of Cornerstone's leadership team remained solid, I often felt like the outsider to conversations in the cabinet. Cornerstone was a multifaceted institution that relied on a variety of revenue streams, including a radio station, a seminary, and professional and graduate programs. For me, the ideal university was one with more of a liberal arts focus, slightly wider theological boundaries, and professors who were first-rate scholars as well as teachers. One institution that fit that mold happened to be just a few miles down the Beltline.

As it turned out, in 2013, Calvin College had a new president who was looking for a provost. I couldn't help but be intrigued, but the idea of a provost at Cornerstone publicly interviewing for the provost position at Calvin would have been out of the question. Calvin, however, promised to run a confidential search process, and so I decided to explore the possibility. In my mind at the time, serving as provost at the college that epitomized the Christian scholarly enterprise—and the former institution of my mentor, George Marsden—seemed a fitting culmination to my academic career. Calvin was interested in the prospect as well, and I had a final interview in February of 2014. A few days later, I traveled to Thailand for meetings with other international educators. Eleven time zones from Michigan, I spent my nights lying half asleep in a Bangkok hotel room, waiting for an email that would affirm my new destiny as provost of Calvin College. The email never came. Calvin's president, an outsider to the institution and the Christian Reformed denomination, wisely chose an internal candidate who had a long history with the institution.

I continued my work at Cornerstone the following year, but the Calvin search process had opened my mind to the possibility of other opportunities. The following fall, Pepperdine University contacted me about applying for the position of dean of Seaver College, the institution's residential undergraduate enterprise, and I responded. Clearly I had gotten on a list of "up and comers" in Christian higher education. A few months later, Lonnie and I traveled to Pepperdine, where I interviewed as a finalist for the position. Pepperdine's stunning Malibu seaside campus and first-rate facilities were a far cry from Cornerstone University, a contrast made even starker because our visit was in February, during the heart of the West Michigan winter. With a highly selective student body; study-abroad sites in Florence, London, and Shanghai; and a basketball team that played Gonzaga and UCLA, this was Christian higher education on a level that I hadn't experienced, and the prospect was intoxicating. Once again, I waited for the notification that never came, and eventually I was informed that Pepperdine had selected an internal candidate. I resigned myself to remaining at Cornerstone, but my passion for the job was waning.

A few weeks later, however, I was contacted by Shirley Hoogstra, who had left Calvin the previous summer to become president of the Council for Christian Colleges & Universities. I had become more involved in the CCCU during my time at Cornerstone and regularly attended its professional conferences. In addition, in the course of expanding study-abroad participation at Cornerstone, I had become familiar with the CCCU's semester-abroad programs and had visited their sites in Oxford and Uganda. Shirley informed me that she was creating a new position at the CCCU—essentially that of a chief academic officer for the organization, overseeing study-abroad, professional development programs for administrators, and grant programs for faculty. The position seemed ideal for me, and after some interviews and a visit to the home office in Washington, DC, I was offered the position.

As in 2009, the timing seemed right for such a move. While Lonnie and I enjoyed living in Grand Rapids, after six years in the provost role, I was growing weary of managing the friction—real or potential—between the institutional gears. And while I could support the university's positions and long-term goals, I wondered if Cornerstone might be better served by a provost who could more enthusiastically champion its commitment to graduate and professional programs. Also, as the human sexuality issue continued to grow in importance on Christian college campuses, I wondered how long a provost with a gay son would be a good fit for a school like Cornerstone. Moreover, I was truly excited about the prospect of working with over a hundred colleges instead of just one, and of overseeing study-abroad programs on six different continents. I met with Joe in May and informed him that I would be leaving Cornerstone for the CCCU.

ooooo

Despite the challenges that accompany being a private university in the Midwest, after my departure Cornerstone University chugged along under Joe Stowell's leadership, erecting a new science building, launching an honors program, and managing to avoid the public controversies that can beset evangelical institutions. The relative calm, however, didn't last. Joe retired in spring 2021. After a national search, in July the Executive Committee of the Board named Gerson Moreno-Riano, former provost at Regent University, as its next president. In the later years of Stowell's presidency, Cornerstone moved toward an increased emphasis on diversity and racial justice, subjects that in today's politically charged environment rival homosexuality in their potential to ignite controversy. The new president reversed the movement toward diversity, and his top-down approach and conservative theological orientation led to several terminations and resignations in his first two months. In October, one day before Moreno-Riano's inauguration ceremony, the Cornerstone faculty, by a 43–6 vote, took the unprecedented step of issuing a statement of no confidence in the new president.

The Board of Trustees, however, doubled down on their decision, and while acknowledging some "transition" difficulties, continued to support the new president. Moreno-Riano, for his part, declared that Cornerstone University was standing "without compromise" on the Bible, perhaps implying that before his arrival, the institution was somehow soft on biblical authority. By the summer of 2022, over sixty professors and staff members had left Cornerstone. Others resigned themselves to keeping their heads down and playing out the string until retirement.

Perhaps in the current era, in which evangelicals seem increasingly attracted to appeals to stand on traditional values against apostasy, institutions that play the "no compromise" card may tap new funding streams and applicant pools. But I wonder about the effects on the health and academic quality of the institution. Indeed, what saddens me most when institutions such as Cornerstone experience turmoil is that professors—the heart of the institution—often end up feeling marginalized and powerless. While in some instances it might be frivolous, in many cases, issuing a vote of no confidence is an act of desperation by professors who feel that they have no other recourse. When nothing tangible results, those who cannot leave tend to go to work, teach their classes, and check their hearts at the door.

I recently read Ann Patchett's novel *Bel Canto*, in which a group of wealthy guests attending a private performance by a famous soprano in a South American country are taken hostage by leftist guerrillas. As the hostage standoff drags on, the opera singer resumes her voice rehearsals, which mesmerizes both the hostages and their captors and improves the morale of the group. Seeking to leverage this benefit, one of the guerrilla leaders, General Hector, declares, "We will make her sing more, and we will tell her what to sing as well." To which the other leader, General Benjamin, replies, "I don't think we should ask."

"We won't be asking," Hector replies, "we will be telling."

Benjamin replies, "Music, I believe, is different. We have set this up exactly right, but if we were to push, we could wind up with nothing."

"If we put a gun to her head she would sing all day."

"Try it first with a bird," Benjamin replies.[10]

Hopefully our institutions don't resemble hostage standoffs, but I couldn't help thinking of an academic community and some of the debates over programs and policies that I've experienced over the years. Theoretically, an institution has the power to tell its employees what to do. But our "product," if you will, is more like music than widgets, and true music can't simply be coerced. If faculty are teaching simply to earn a paycheck rather than out of a true sense of calling and partnership with the administration, then like a soprano forced to sing at gunpoint, the heart of the enterprise has been lost.

∞∞∞

When I left Cornerstone in the summer of 2015, however, that unexpected turmoil was far off in the school's future. While we had a few mini-dramas of our own and some setbacks, Cornerstone overall was a place where good academic work happened, lives were changed for the better, and I got to play a part in that process. I prefer to conclude this chapter, therefore, not with controversy but with a vignette of a perfect day in the life of a provost.

It's a frigid Friday morning in January. I leave for work in the dark at 7:15, the Beltline sporting a new layer of overnight lake-effect snow. My 2004 Nissan Sentra is basically a sled on four wheels, which means that I need to perfectly time my "Michigan left turn"—which is actually a U-turn—into Cornerstone so that I carry momentum through the plowed snow that has accumulated in the turnaround lanes. I arrive at 7:30 and answer emails in a dark office with my desk light on as daylight grows outside my window. The old administration building heats poorly, so like most employees, I have a banned space heater quietly humming under my desk.

Liz comes in around 8:00 and we discuss the day ahead. At 9:00 I drop in on Gail Duhon, the registrar. She laments my latest crazy initiative to remake the university—a four-day class week proposal with Wednesday serving as a midweek "quiet day"—and what that would mean for her staff's workload. Gail's complaining is only in jest, however; she and Liz actually appreciate most of my quirks and are my biggest supporters among the staff.

At 9:30, I prepare, logistically and psychologically, for the faculty meeting, which takes place at 10:00 a.m. one Friday per month. The agenda is set in advance in coordination with Faculty Senate, and everything is in place. But the faculty meeting begins with open Q&A with the president, and one never knows where the conversation might go during that time. Liz provides Starbucks and fresh donuts, however, which puts the faculty in a positive mood. I count the faculty meeting a success if I manage to stand in the back for most of the meeting and let professors drive the agenda and discussion, a significant improvement from the previous era of death-by-PowerPoint faculty meetings. I squeeze in two division chair visits between the faculty meeting and lunch, following my usual routine of thirty-minute check-in meetings every two weeks. And I always let the chair lead off; my agenda items come second.

I arrive at the Dining Commons at 12:15, just after the student rush at noon, to see what the barbarians have left from the salad and pasta bars. Lunch for faculty and staff is two dollars for all you can eat. Thus, true to my Dutch heritage, I attempt to cram an entire day's worth of food consumption into lunch. The attempt is made more difficult since trays have been banned from campus, both because students were piling them up with too much extra food and because they tended to disappear from the dining room on good sledding days. I squeeze myself into a table of seven professors at the northwest corner of the Dining Commons. This is my opportunity to get faculty feedback about the faculty meeting and learn what questions were left unanswered.

Then it's time to tour campus. I've developed a circuit after lunch that takes me through every faculty and academic building on the way back to my office (it's a small campus). I head south out of the Student Center and enter the Faculty Office Building, a.k.a. Fowler's Folly, home to the Humanities and Bible Divisions. I drop in on a few professors before ending up at the corner office occupied by Matt Bonzo, the Wendell Berry–reading head of the Institute for Christianity and Cultural Engagement, which boasts the memorable acronym of ICCE (pronounced "Icky"). Matt is a friend and trusted advisor whom I count on to convey the unvarnished truth about the faculty culture.

I head south out of the FOB, then enter the back door of the Teacher Education Building, walking the long hallway and greeting whoever happens to be in. From there I head up to the new chapel. It's empty on a Friday afternoon, and standing in the middle of the building and turning slowly, I can admire all four of the building's stunning stained glass windows, courtesy of Roberta Ahmanson. Then I head north to the Bolthouse Building, home of the Business and Communications Divisions and several classrooms. I make the rounds through the business faculty offices, making sure to visit Larry Bos, a thirty-five-year veteran and the unofficial leader of the faculty. I quietly wander through the halls and listen in on afternoon classes in session. For a provost, there's no better experience than eavesdropping on classes, knowing that you're doing the grunt work, and sometimes the dirty work, so that the real business of the university, teaching and learning, can flourish.

Finally, I head through the Daverman Science Building, home to the young-earth creationist professors who are also some of the most kind-hearted, long-suffering faculty on campus. Their embarrassingly subpar facilities, which the Admissions Department carefully bypasses during campus tours, will be replaced with a new building two years after my departure, a final benefit of Joe's diligent fund-raising efforts.

I head back to my office for a quiet afternoon of emails, preparing reports, and other paperwork. From a wise provost colleague, Linda Samek, I learned the habit of not scheduling meetings on Friday afternoons in order to recover, regroup, and make sense of the week. Joe drops in at 3:00 to debrief, get my take on how the faculty meeting went, and wish me a good weekend. I don't begrudge him the early departure, since he will host an alumni event in Detroit on Saturday, preach in a local church on Sunday, and show up in the office on Monday morning as fresh as ever.

At 4:00, I leave the office and head to my customary spot— the window table at Starbucks in Gaslight Village in East Grand Rapids. The January sun (what there is of it) in Michigan sets early, and the softening light on the sidewalk snow outside my window is my favorite scene of the week. Using notes that I've jotted in my laptop throughout the week, I compose my weekly Provost's Update. At 5:15, I email the update to Lonnie. She's playing piano for classes at the Grand Rapids Ballet but has the remarkable ability to proofread emails while playing. A few minutes later she emails me back, correcting typos and altering overly cynical passages. At 5:30, I send out the revised email and blind-copy Joe, following my policy of never sending any public communication that doesn't include the president.

At 5:45, I leave Starbucks and walk a half block to Olive's Restaurant for happy hour. A pint of Bell's Two-Hearted for five dollars is what makes Grand Rapids the great city that it is. Lonnie arrives from the ballet and meets me there, and if we're lucky, the high-top table at the window next to the bar will be open. And if we're even luckier, snowflakes will be falling gently in the glow of the streetlights, a fitting ending to a week blessed by good and meaningful work.

SIX

Plot Twist

IN THE SUMMER OF 2015, we sold our white house with the big front porch in East Grand Rapids and moved into a brick row-house at 807 Massachusetts Avenue NE, Washington, DC, two blocks from the Council for Christian Colleges & Universities' home office on Capitol Hill. If East Grand Rapids had reminded us of Europe, Capitol Hill, with its old rowhouses set behind tiny yards and its shaded sidewalks—and with Eastern Market a short walk away—did so even more. On the way to Washington, we dropped off Anna at Lee University in Tennessee for her freshman year of college. Becoming empty nesters thus joined the summer's list of significant life changes, along with selling a house, moving cross-country, and beginning a new job. On my first day of work, eager to make a good first impression, I rose early and arrived in my new office at 7:15 a.m. For the next ninety minutes I worked alone, wondering if I had accidentally begun on a holiday, before other employees began trickling in. It was my first lesson that in the nation's capital, the workday starts later and ends later, if it ends at all.

∞∞∞

In order to understand the Council for Christian Colleges & Universities, we must take a step back and survey the world of higher-education associations. Private colleges and universities have split personalities. While fiercely independent and competitive, they also long for connection and maintain a tribal solidarity in relation to larger public universities. Thus, an alphabet soup of association acronyms has accumulated in private higher education over the past century.

The typical private college is a member of the Council of Independent Colleges (CIC) and the National Association of Independent Colleges & Universities (NAICU). But that's just at the national level. A host of regional associations vie for colleges' loyalty as well. Most states have an independent college association, and those are matched by trans-state organizations such as the Appalachian Colleges Association. Some associations welcome all comers, while others are more selective. The Great Lakes College Association, for example, consists of traditional elite liberal arts colleges such as Kenyon, Oberlin, and Wabash and would not think of including less traditional institutions such as Indiana Wesleyan. At Cornerstone, we were members of the Michigan Independent Colleges and Universities (MICU) but couldn't join the Michigan Colleges Alliance (MCA) because Cornerstone wasn't part of the original fourteen-member group when the organization was formed decades earlier.

Then there are associations based on distinct institutional identities, such as the Yes We Can Coalition, which consists of private institutions that enroll a higher percentage of Pell-eligible students. And there are several associations based on religious identity. Catholic institutions have the Association of Catholic Colleges and Universities, Bible colleges have the Association for Biblical Higher Education (ABHE), and Seventh-day Adventist institutions have the Association of Adventist Colleges and Universities, just to name a few.

The result is a dizzying array of overlapping memberships and affiliations. To take one example: Calvin University belongs to regional associations such as MICU and MCA and national associations such as CIC and NAICU. In addition, because of its religious identity, it belongs to the Council for Christian Colleges & Universities (more on that soon) as well as the Association of Reformed Colleges and Universities.

It's a highly competitive market—most associations subsist on membership fees and conference revenue, after all—so associations must demonstrate that they provide something of value to justify the membership fee. Since the decision to join often rests with presidents and cabinet-level officers, associations typically hold their annual meetings for these individuals during the winter in warm climates, which tips the scales strongly in favor of membership. State associations typically justify their value by advocating in the state government for private higher-education funding. The ABHE has a strong card to play in that it also serves as the accrediting body for most of its members. Others, such as the CIC, excel in providing professional development programs for faculty and administrators.

Then there's the Council for Christian Colleges & Universities. In the mid-twentieth century, Christian colleges, reflecting the evangelical movement in general, began to expand in size and quality. As they did, they sought to collaborate with other like-minded institutions. In 1971, ten colleges joined to form the Christian College Consortium. It was an eclectic assortment of Christian institutions including some of the more prominent Christian colleges (Wheaton and Taylor) and others that were less well known (Eastern Mennonite and Malone).

The Consortium hosted some events for members focusing on the topic of integrating faith and learning. These meetings attracted the interest of other evangelical colleges, but the presidents of the original institutions were reluctant to expand. At the same time, Christian colleges were growing increasingly concerned about expanded federal involvement in higher education, such as Title IX regulations regarding gender discrimination and the impending creation of a cabinet-level Department of Education. As a result, in 1976, several college leaders gathered to create a second organization, the Christian College Coalition (its name would eventually be changed to the Council for Christian Colleges & Universities). It established its headquarters in Washington, DC, and announced a primary purpose of advocating for faith-based higher education. The new organization distanced itself from Bible colleges by requiring that members be accredited institutions offering degrees in the arts and sciences. In addition to political advocacy, the CCCU organized professional development activities for members, fostered institutional collaboration, and eventually created several semester-abroad programs.

Christian colleges and universities generally prospered from the late 1970s to early in the decade 2000–2009, and the CCCU benefited from the movement's expansion. From 38 original members in 1976, the organization grew to 120 members in 2010—including 25 members outside of North America—and attracted prominent institutions such as Baylor University and Pepperdine University as partial members. Overall, the organization ran smoothly until 2013, when Ed Blews, the former president of the MICU, succeeded Paul Corts as president. Blews's presidency was marked by internal disarray and the departure of several key staff members, and he and the CCCU parted ways after six months. Chip Pollard, president of John Brown University, was serving as board chair at the time, and under the leadership of Chip and interim president Bill Robinson, the CCCU managed to host a successful International Forum on Christian Higher Education in Los Angeles in March 2014 amid the turmoil.

A few months later, the CCCU board named Shirley Hoogstra as the new president. If they hoped that the new president would infuse new optimism and energy into the organization, they seemed to have found the right person. Shirley is one of those tall, blonde-haired, energetic Dutch women that abound in West Michigan. She grew up in Holland, Michigan, the daughter of the owner of the local hardware store. Shirley graduated from Calvin College, began her professional career as a grade school teacher, then eventually earned a JD at the University of Connecticut. She practiced law in Connecticut for thirteen years before moving with her husband, Jeff, to Grand Rapids, where she served as Calvin's vice president for student development for fifteen years.

With her extensive professional background and confident demeanor, Shirley was perfectly suited to holding her own in a room full of alpha male (and a few alpha female) college presidents. Since her family was based in Grand Rapids, Shirley bought a second home on Capitol Hill near the CCCU office and set about revitalizing the organization. By the time I joined in summer 2015, she had hired a new chief financial officer from North Carolina, Walter Miller, and promoted Shapri LoMaglio, a staff member who had persisted through the Blews presidency, to vice president for Government and External Relations. I joined the team as vice president for Academic Affairs and Professional Programs.

∞∞∞∞

After serving as provost at Cornerstone for six years, wondering when underlying tensions over evolution, human sexuality, or faculty parking might boil to the surface, I looked forward to the relative calm of working for a small organization in Washington, DC. My new colleague, Shapri, assured me that August was the CCCU's quiet month, as member schools busily prepared for the new academic year. Instead, the summer of 2015 turned out to be one of the most contentious and pivotal seasons of the CCCU's forty-year history.

On June 26, the Supreme Court, in *Obergefell v. Hodges*, legalized same-sex marriage and required all states to recognize its legitimacy. The ruling essentially brought the LGBTQ issue to the CCCU's front doorstep and threatened to split the organization. One key to the CCCU's growth over the decades has been that, unlike other cooperative movements such as the National Association of Evangelicals, it requires no doctrinal statement for membership. Members must simply have a board-approved, publicly stated Christian mission and hire only Christians as full-time faculty and staff. But defining the exact nature of its Christian identity is left up to each institution.

These minimal requirements enabled the CCCU to expand to include institutions from thirty-seven different denominations. But they also meant that underneath the surface of the CCCU, combustible ingredients existed that could ignite under the right conditions. Concerning marriage, in 2001, then-president Robert Andringa appointed a Task Force on Human Sexuality. The group anchored the CCCU's own hiring policy, student programs, and public advocacy in a traditional view of marriage as "a sacred union between a man and a woman." Anticipating the importance of the issue in the decades to come, the task force also urged each member institution to "decide its stance on this difficult issue explicitly and deliberately."[11] Was the CCCU home office's view of marriage shared by all of the members of the organization? Time would tell.

Across the spectrum of the CCCU, the Mennonite schools have tended to interpret Scripture differently than do institutions with Baptist or Reformed orientations. Taking the Sermon on the Mount as normative, the Mennonite churches and schools have historically been pacifist, whereas many Christian colleges have emphasized patriotism and supported the US military. Also, emphasizing the inclusion of socially marginalized groups, many Mennonite institutions have taken a less oppositional stance on homosexuality. After *Obergefell v. Hodges*, therefore, two Mennonite members, Eastern Mennonite University (EMU) and Goshen College, changed their policy to permit the hiring of any Christian in a legal marriage, whether heterosexual or same-sex. Their decision alarmed some conservative CCCU members. Oklahoma Wesleyan University president Everett Piper and Union University president Dub Oliver publicly demanded that the CCCU take action to oust what they viewed as the heretical institutions. The controversy attracted the keen interest of the conservative editors at *World* magazine, who provided Piper and Oliver with a public platform to air their views.

By the time of the annual meeting of the CCCU board of directors at Lake Geneva, Wisconsin, in late July, a potential public relations crisis was brewing, and Oklahoma Baptist and Union were threatening to leave the CCCU if it did not take action soon. The meeting was my first event with the CCCU, and, ironically, EMU president Loren Swartzendruber was a member of the board. Loren, a kind, mild-mannered gentleman, and his wife chatted with Lonnie and me during an evening boat ride around the lake, and

I mused that he seemed an unlikely person to bear the mantle of undermining the foundations of Christian higher education.

The same-sex marriage issue co-opted much of the board meeting. The first priority was to issue a public statement that would reassure members of the CCCU's commitment to biblical orthodoxy, and buy some time for calm and reasoned deliberation among the members. Shapri and I drafted a statement in the hotel restaurant, which Shirley and the board revised, approved, and issued on July 28. In it, the board announced that it would embark on "a deliberative and consultative process" of personally calling all 120 CCCU presidents to discuss the issue. The statement went on to affirm that "the vast majority of member schools hold to a historic, orthodox understanding of marriage between a man and a woman."[12] For conservative schools, however, that was the rub: a "vast majority" implies that some members of the organization do not hold to that position, which others perceived as an essential plank of the faith. Was the CCCU as an organization committed to a traditional view of marriage or not? One conservative president urged the board to "act courageously and act quickly."

In the month after the board meeting, board members divided up the list of college presidents and called each individual to get his or her feedback. In early August, Union and Oklahoma Wesleyan left the organization and publicly decried its lack of biblical conviction. Calling the event the CCCU's greatest crisis, *World* magazine claimed that a significant number of the organization's members were contemplating leaving. EMU and Goshen, desiring to not be a source of division but remain in the organization, offered to move to "affiliate" status as a compromise measure, but no action was taken at the time.

The board completed its calls to presidents in early September, and a week later, Shirley and board chair Chip Pollard held a conference call to update members on the results. Predictably, responses were mixed. Roughly 70 percent of the membership agreed in full or in principle with EMU and Goshen remaining in the organization as affiliate members, 10 percent believed they should remain as full members, and 20 percent wanted them out of the organization completely.

Chip also announced that EMU and Goshen had decided to withdraw completely from the CCCU, both because they did not want to serve as a cause of division in the organization, and out of a desire to pursue a more progressive form of Christian higher education. The immediate cause of controversy, therefore, was removed, but the question regarding the CCCU and same-sex marriage was unresolved. Thus, Chip announced, the CCCU was creating a task force to review the criteria for membership to "explore categories for affiliation that would enable the CCCU to remain rooted in historic Christianity while also being a broadly inclusive association that welcomes other Christian institutions seeking to advance the cause of Christian higher education."[13]

The task force was chaired by two board members—Barry Corey, president of Biola University, and Phil Ryken, president of Wheaton College—and consisted of twelve other presidents. It included a broad cross section of membership, from Dallas Theological Seminary president Mark Bailey to Pepperdine University president Andrew Benson. After several months of deliberation, the group issued a report to the board in July 2016. The board in turn made some minor revisions and issued the approved report to the membership in September.

Since 1995, the CCCU had included an "affiliate" membership class to incorporate a variety of institutions that were committed to Christian higher education but did not fully align with the CCCU's membership criteria. Those included, for example, Bible colleges and seminaries that differed from the organization academically and schools such as Pepperdine that hired some non-Christian professors in particular professional areas. Now the membership categories were expanded to include the possible half-membership of schools with more progressive views on same-sex marriage. To do so, the task force identified six general criteria for membership. Items such as a publicly stated Christian mission, regional accreditation, nonprofit status, financial integrity, and a Christians-only hiring policy were basically a continuation of previous standards.

The main addition was number six, "Christian Distinctives and Advocacy," which identified a number of positions that the CCCU advocated for. Couched among statements about environmental stewardship, caring for the poor, and racial reconciliation was the key statement on marriage: "We hold the Christian belief that human beings, male and female, are created in the image of God to flourish in community, and, as to intimate sexual relations, they are intended for persons in a marriage between one man and one woman."[14]

Institutions that aligned with all six criteria, including the traditional view of marriage, were designated "Governing Members" and were eligible to vote for members of the board of directors. A second class of membership, "Associate Members," were institutions that shared the same theological commitments but were not accredited undergraduate institutions with majors in the arts and sciences, such as seminaries and Bible colleges. A third group, "Collaborative Partners," consisted of schools that either did not restrict hiring to professing Christian faculty and staff *or* did not maintain institutional practices that aligned with the marriage statement. Associate Members and Collaborative Partners were not eligible to vote for CCCU board members, but otherwise they were free to participate in all the other CCCU programs and activities.

The solution wasn't perfect, and some noted that it seemed to relegate some of the organization's most prominent members such as Baylor and Pepperdine to second-class status. It did, however, strike a balance between traditional biblical orthodoxy and inclusivity, a balance that has held up quite well so far. Some long-standing members, such as Seattle Pacific University and Whitworth University, eventually moved to Collaborative Partner status because of the new membership framework, while Cedarville University and the Master's College and Seminary left the organization over concerns about doctrinal orthodoxy. But their departures have been outweighed by new additions, and the overall membership has grown to over 185 institutions worldwide. The CCCU can rightly claim, as it does on its website, that it is the leading national voice of Christian higher education in America. Whether any further unraveling of American evangelicalism will affect the tenuous unity of the CCCU is yet to be seen.

ooooo

By the time the task force had completed its work, I had settled into my role as vice president. Because it consists of nearly two hundred colleges and universities, the CCCU might seem to outsiders like a large organization. The reality, however, is that only about twenty-five employees worked in the home office in DC and another fifty or so worked off-site at semester-abroad programs. Compared to even a small college, the CCCU felt more like a small tech start-up. Despite its small scale, the CCCU occupies prime real estate in Washington, DC. In the 1980s, when Capitol Hill was known for its crack houses and property was cheap, the CCCU's leaders wisely scrounged enough cash together to purchase three adjoining buildings on Eighth Street Northeast. Washington architecture being what it is, the main building is a fifteen-foot-wide rowhouse with four floors of small offices stacked on top of each other and connected by a central stairwell. The middle building is a forty-bed dormitory that houses the American Studies Program, the CCCU's first semester-abroad program, started in the 1970s. The third building, a redbrick rowhouse, holds a classroom and administrative offices for the semester-abroad programs. The space is more open and conducive to interaction, and since most of my time would be spent overseeing study abroad (and I dislike cramped spaces), that's where I soon moved my office.

Semester-abroad programs comprise their own peculiar subculture in American higher education. For students, they can be disorienting and stressful but also life-transforming. Far from the home campus and embedded in a foreign culture, such programs require an unusual set of skills to create and operate successfully. The typical program director is a one-person university who, when called to do so, can function as professor, dean, registrar, chaplain, resident director, recruiter, and disciplinarian. Often more at home in a foreign country than in the United States, directors can be eccentric and highly independent, accustomed to running their operations free of interference from meddling, small-minded administrators back in the States.

The CCCU had its fair share of study-abroad program directors with colorful personalities. Although we mostly conversed by Skype and rarely met in person, many of them, in addition to being my subordinates, also became my friends, confidants, and advisors. Among them were Oxford Studies director Stan Rosenberg, my UK cycling companion, single-malt aficionado, and a tireless promoter of all things British; Uganda Studies director Rachel Robinson, an artistic, soft-spoken Mary Oliver devotee who became a spiritual mentor to our daughter Anna; Doug and Patti Magnuson, who persisted in leading a Middle East Studies program that moved from Cairo to Jerusalem to Jordan in search of a stable home base; and Nashville Music Center director Warren Pettit, a Canadian-born gun rights advocate whose program launched countless CCCU students into the music industry. Australian Studies Center director Kimberly Spragg, a bubbly Texan and social progressive, was Warren's polar opposite on the political spectrum, but the two were best friends at our annual meetings.

The turmoil in the CCCU's recent years had been particularly hard on the directors' morale, and some of them wondered whether study-abroad programs had a future in the organization. I made it a primary goal to value the directors and make them feel that the home office supported them. At the same time, I sought to develop a greater sense of consistency across the programs by articulating some common goals shared by all the programs and by developing a common end-of-semester program evaluation. Unfortunately, as academic vice president for what was essentially a Christian college spread out over six continents, my job also required some of the typically difficult decisions that leaders sometimes have to make. In my first year, we closed the China Studies program due to low enrollment, and we made other personnel changes over the years. International travel is great, except when the purpose of the trip is to personally deliver bad news to good people. Finally, recognizing the difficulty and geographical isolation of the directors' work, we included plenty of time for fellowship and relaxation at our annual directors' meetings. Nothing boosts morale like ample supplies of good food and drinks on the large back patio of a vacation rental in suburban Washington.

Like the CIC, the CCCU provided professional development programs for professors and academic administrators, and much of that responsibility fell to me. For example, partnering with David Smith at Calvin College, we restarted the New Faculty Institute—the same one I had attended twenty years earlier as a young professor. Another rewarding task was to strengthen a sense of esprit de corps among my former peer group, the chief academic officers. One way to do so was simply to get out on the road and visit campuses. I enjoyed traveling to CCCU members in urban centers like Minneapolis-St. Paul and Los Angeles as well as to pockets of schools in more rural regions such as northwest Iowa and northern Indiana.

The typical Christian college provost, like the CCCU semester-abroad program directors scattered around the world, can experience a similar feeling of isolation both geographically and institutionally. After all, there's only one provost per college. Thus, I adapted my weekly provost update from Cornerstone days into a "CCCU update" that I emailed to 120 chief academic officers across the country. Once again, as at Cornerstone, I discovered that regular, predictable written communication, sprinkled with general reflections, sarcasm, and encouragement, can strengthen bonds across distance. Late Friday afternoon resumed its place in my weekly schedule as a time for writing updates—one week's email going to my CCCU semester program directors, the next week's going to CCCU provosts.

ooooo

While work at the CCCU was going well, life in Washington was difficult for Lonnie and me. Moving from a faculty to an administrative role at a university is a significant change; moving from administrator at a university to staff member at a member services organization is another shift. It can feel like yet another step further away from the primary work of education that happens in the classroom, the laboratory, and the dormitory. I had moved from being on a campus supporting professors in their roles to working in a small office in Washington, DC, where the nearest CCCU campus was a couple of hours away. Moreover, my primary peer group—cynical middle-aged academics—was noticeably absent from the organization. I enjoyed visiting college campuses but always recognized that I was a guest at the dinner table, not a member of the family. My former colleague Ed Ericson once suggested that, because of its isolation from the real world of academics, the CCCU academic vice president position should rotate among provosts—kind of like a temporary department chair position in which each professor "takes one for the team" and fills in at some point. His words were beginning to resonate with me.

Lonnie too was struggling in her own way. With Anna off to college, her identity for the past twenty-five years as mother to four children was fundamentally altered. Also, professional piano work was difficult to obtain in Washington because area universities relied on ample supplies of graduate students for such work. Thus, while I was busy in the office or out traveling, Lonnie was often left at home alone without significant work and far from family and friends. And while Capitol Hill is a charming neighborhood, it tends to be populated either by retired government officials or by young professional families who eventually move to the suburbs once their children reach school age. What Lonnie and I valued most about Siloam Springs and Grand Rapids, a sense of community, was difficult to find on Capitol Hill.

After several months in Washington, we visited a family friend who served as a Michigan representative in Congress. Like many politicians, he spent his weekdays in Washington and flew home for the weekends. An idea lodged in my head, and a few days later I showed Lonnie a house for sale on Zillow: it was a lovely little white house on Argentina Drive in East Grand Rapids, about five blocks away from our earlier house on Lake Drive. What initially seemed like a crazy idea became more reasonable when we considered Michigan's lower cost of living, the ability of Lonnie to have her piano work again, and the opportunity to inhabit once again a vibrant community in Grand Rapids. Plus, we had a solid relationship based on over thirty years of marriage; we could handle being apart during the workweek. But it was a big step, and would mean a different lifestyle for both of us. In June, at a CCCU event in Washington State, as I wrestled with the alternatives, I sent Lonnie a simple text: "Where would you rather live, DC or GR?" She replied, "GR." That same day, a trusted and godly friend from Arkansas texted me, "Go for it! Do it!" I had never relied on divine messages in a smart phone, but this seemed like a good time to start.

Thus began an unusual but rewarding new stage of life as I belatedly discovered single living in middle age. Doug Koopman, a Calvin College political science professor, was doing a one-year sabbatical in the District, and he found a one-bedroom "English basement" apartment, as they are known, on Independence Avenue, just three blocks from Congress. Doug rigged up a Murphy bed for me in the living room. Our routines meshed pretty well, except for Doug's habit of rising at 5:00 a.m. to work out in a nearby gym, which, despite his best efforts, usually entailed waking me up on his way out. I would return the favor when I entered the apartment at 10:30 p.m. after working from the patio of the nearby National Archives building.

After Doug's sabbatical ended, I found a new arrangement. Scanning Airbnb, Lonnie noticed an upstairs bedroom available in a house on Ninth Street Northeast, just two blocks from the CCCU office, and inquired if the owners would be interested in renting out the bedroom by the month. The co-owners, Jen and Genie, agreed. So began my "Three's Company" life stage in the upstairs bedroom of two working professionals on Capitol Hill. Such pragmatic arrangements, while odd by Midwestern standards, are not unusual in cities with absurdly high housing costs such as Washington. Jen, Genie, the two residents of their English basement, and I became friends, and of course the extrovert Lonnie was a popular addition on her occasional visits to Washington. I was not a fan of their two cats, who were fond of sneaking into my bedroom during the workday and leaving their long hair on my bed, but I did my part in parceling out the appropriate portions of gourmet canned cat food in their bowls when Jen and Genie were out of town.

As far as the commute, my routine was actually easier than most inter-city commuters, since Grand Rapids and Washington share the same time zone and a direct flight between the airports takes seventy-five minutes. Thus, on a typical Monday, I would grab the 7:00 a.m. American Airlines flight out of Grand Rapids (seat 2A with a Grande Starbucks is the perfect way to begin the week), land at Ronald Reagan National Airport around 8:30, order an Uber while deplaning, and arrive in the office along with the rest of the staff around 9:15.

The return on Thursday or Friday evening was more onerous: Reagan Airport contained Gate 35X, which was not actually a gate but just an entry point to several gates on the airport's ground level. Around 5:00 p.m. each workday, American Airlines scheduled a fleet of puddle-jumpers to depart Reagan for second-tier cities such as Albany, Greensboro, and Grand Rapids. Travelers waited in the crowded upper floor until their city was called on a muffled loudspeaker, then descended the escalator and boarded their assigned bus, which dodged gasoline trucks and luggage carts while negotiating its way to the appropriate plane out on the tarmac. It was all quite chaotic, and more than once, while settling into my seat, the pilot would announce the destination city, and a traveler would jump up and rush out of the plane. If all went well, I would arrive in Grand Rapids by 7:00, in time for a late dinner.

During the workweek itself, I learned to buy and prepare food—things that I had done little of in our fairly traditional marriage. Trader Joe's on Eighth and Pennsylvania became my best friend, and my penchant for routine took over: spaghetti, broccoli, and spinach salad for dinner; granola, coffee, and orange juice for breakfast; half of a banana at midmorning; leftover spaghetti and yogurt for lunch; coffee at 4:00 p.m.; repeat. Like my eating, my work life settled into a predictable routine as well: I arrived at the office at 7:30, courtesy of a one-minute commute, and worked until 5:00 p.m. Then I took a one-hour bike ride on the Anacostia River trail northeast toward Baltimore and back, highlighted by a sprint down East Capitol and a descent down the steep hill on the north side of the Capitol building. Threading the vehicle barriers below the Capitol at twenty-five miles per hour was a great closing adrenaline rush to my ride. After dinner and Facetime with Lonnie, I returned to work on the front porch swing, which served as my home office during the warm summer evenings. With a job that combined oversight of nine semester-abroad programs and professional development for the organization, I never ran out of things to do, and what my week may have lacked in work-life balance, it made up for in distraction-free productivity.

Ironically, my single lifestyle during the week enabled me to be more closely involved with my CCCU staff colleagues. Most of the semester-abroad staff were recent college graduates, but they generously welcomed a middle-aged professional into the club. Over lunch we would hang out on the back patio, watch *Extreme Home Makeover*, or sometimes head up to the rooftop patio of the dormitory for views of the Capitol Dome to the west. Occasionally we would enjoy happy hour at Kenny's Barbecue a block from the office, drinking local brews out of plastic cups on the patio. One of the staff members, Jordan, was also a cocktail aficionado, and he gave me the ultimate sign of acceptance by naming an original drink after me.

Occasionally, Lonnie and I would reverse the routine and she would visit Washington for the weekend. While Grand Rapids was our chosen home, we loved spending time together in the Capital, where we could meet friends for dinner, stroll Eastern Market on Saturday morning, bike in Rock Creek Park, drop into the National Art Gallery for a walk through the French Impressionism rooms, catch a free concert at the Navy Yard park, attend church at St. Peter's, and read the Sunday *New York Times* at Radici's coffee shop. Washington, DC, didn't work well as our primary home, but it was unbeatable for monthly weekend getaways.

ooooo

As I forged a new lifestyle as a long-distance commuter, my work at the CCCU itself became increasingly stressful. The semester programs were the financial lifeblood of the CCCU, and their enrollment was lagging. Study-abroad programs operate downstream from colleges and universities and depend on the health of those institutions for survival. CCCU institutions need to be willing to send their students—and their tuition dollars—off-campus for a semester. In the 1980s and 1990s, Christian colleges were growing, and the CCCU's programs benefited from the spillover. New programs were created, enrollments grew, and study abroad served as a cash cow for the organization. As CCCU members became more financially stressed, and especially after the recession of 2008, many college leaders became increasingly reluctant to see their tuition dollars going to Oxford, Uganda, or Costa Rica. One administrator informed me that CCCU programs were a "cannibal" on his institution. My typical response to challenges, whether painting a three-story house, biking up a mountain, or running a university, had always been to work harder. But this was a challenge that couldn't simply be surmounted by working longer and harder.

Furthermore, in the heightened political environment for Christian higher education, it seemed that most of my work activities and priorities were increasingly tangential to those of the organization. While study-abroad and professional development programs are nice features, ultimately, joining the CCCU is a decision of the president, and the easiest way to raise a president's temperature is to mention the possibility that the college might forfeit government funding or lose accreditation because of its policies on same-sex marriage. For them, the real value of the CCCU lies in its work defending the religious freedom of Christian institutions, and that value increases the more such freedom is perceived as being under threat.

The CCCU's most important advocacy work was a new initiative called Fairness for All. After the same-sex marriage membership controversy was resolved, the CCCU's advocacy efforts took an ironic turn. Historically, the issues of gay rights and religious freedom had been understood as a zero-sum game: more gay rights means less religious freedom, and vice versa. In Utah, however, politicians took a creative new approach in 2013 that linked the two agendas, which they labeled Fairness for All: they passed a law that simultaneously protected gay and transgender Americans from discrimination in hiring and housing while also encoding faith-based exemptions to protect the right of religious organizations to operate according to their beliefs about sexuality and marriage. Noting its success in Utah, the CCCU promoted the strategy at the federal level.

Fairness for All made good sense both theologically and practically, and one could argue that it paved the way for the eventual passage of the Respect for Marriage act in 2022. Moreover, the advocacy effort itself communicated to a broader audience that evangelicals were not bigots. In a civil society, one way that Christians can love their neighbor is by advocating for basic rights for everyone, regardless of sexual orientation. In fact, some positive relationships developed between the CCCU and gay rights advocates because of the campaign. Coordinating a national political campaign, however, was a huge endeavor for a small organization. Moreover, the initiative was controversial within the CCCU's own ranks and required frequent communication and reassurance to members. I can just imagine a phone conversation between Shirley Hoogstra and a CCCU college president: "So let me get this straight: I'm sending money to the CCCU so that it can advocate on behalf of civil rights for gay people?" Thus, Fairness for All consumed much of the CCCU leadership's time and attention over the next two years.

What all of that meant for me was that other than study-abroad enrollment, which wasn't going well, most of the initiatives that occupied my attention seemed less important to the organization. Moreover, despite our personal friendship, Shirley and I had different approaches to leadership that became more apparent over time. In an organization as small as the CCCU, such differences had little room to dissipate. Finally, there was the strain of a seemingly endless workload in a job that was essentially two previous full-time positions combined into one. By the summer of 2018, I wondered how long I could continue in what had become an emotionally and spiritually draining job. As it turned out, I didn't have to wonder for very long.

ooooo

On August 14, 2018, after two weeks of vacation, I took my customary flight from Grand Rapids to Washington, DC, arriving in Reagan Airport and Ubering to the office in time for the weekly 10:00 a.m. staff meeting. Later that morning, I was informed that I was being reassigned to a new part-time role as vice president for research and scholarship, which I would fulfill from Grand Rapids, and that the position would end the following May. As organizations often do in such situations, it was essentially a termination framed as a lateral move, thereby enabling the person to preserve some professional dignity and provide some lead time to make a job change. My twenty-year climb up the professional ladder of academia was ended, at least for now.

I recalled an article by psychologist Gary Klein about the value of performing what he called a "pre-mortem." We're familiar with a postmortem, in which a coroner examines a dead body to determine the cause of death. Klein suggested that before significant decisions in life or business, we might do well to do a "pre-mortem"—that is, ask ourselves on the front end: If this thing doesn't work out, what will be the cause of death? Doing so, he suggested, might lead us to question taking certain risky steps, or at least to adjust course early in the process. I remembered that article and reflected on the previous three years. Were there any preliminary signs that a "perfect match" may not have been so perfect after all? What went wrong, and why?[15]

Certain things became clearer in hindsight. One was different unstated assumptions about the nature of my role at the organization, which were exacerbated by the decision to live in Grand Rapids. Furthermore, given the financial challenges our member institutions were facing and their impact on CCCU semester-abroad programs, in retrospect, it seemed that what the CCCU really needed was not so much a chief academic officer as a chief *enrollment* officer—someone with experience and expertise in marketing and promotions who could perhaps shore up the declining numbers in our programs. I thrived in the academic role but was slow to adapt to the reality that my job was actually more sales than operations.

Ironically, I would become something of a sales rock star in a future job, but sometimes I'm a slow learner. Finally, the president came from the highly structured worlds of elementary school, law, and student development; I came from academia and was accustomed to leading highly independent professors and program directors with a light touch. The two different approaches in a small organization didn't mesh well. Fond of viewing life in biking terms, I journaled at the time,

> A road bike is a fast machine, but when you put a road bike on a gravel road, its assets can become weaknesses. Sometimes the road unexpectedly changes from pavement to gravel, and you just make the best of it for as long as you can.
>
> A tandem bike can have two strong riders. But the pedal cranks are connected, so if the riders pedal at different cadences, the bike is not effective.

A colleague of mine at Cornerstone University, Gerald Long-john, once wrote an article in the student newspaper about stressful travel situations entitled "If It's Funny Later, It's Funny Now." For example, if you find yourself sleeping overnight in the terminal of Zimbabwe International Airport because Air Zimbabwe canceled your flight, it helps to keep in mind that someday you'll have a great story to tell your friends. Being dismissed from the CCCU wasn't funny at the time, and wasn't funny later. But it did provide me with an unusual plot twist in life and an interesting story, and I like to think that even at the time, I realized that taking the larger perspective and not going rogue on my former organization was the best way through it. I continue to work regularly with the CCCU, and in fact much of my professional success over the past few years has been based on a strong working relationship with the organization. Shirley and I see each other occasionally at conferences, and when we do, we give each other a hug and ask about our families (grandchildren are a great conversation-starter). We both have much to offer Christian higher education, but we make better professional colleagues than we did coworkers.

ooooo

Ironically, that same Monday, I had an afternoon flight to Knoxville, Tennessee, where I was scheduled to lead Carson-Newman University's fall faculty workshop the next day. Since I had been on vacation the previous two weeks, I planned to use the plane ride and time in the hotel to plan my talk. Events of the morning, however, hadn't put me in a good frame of mind for workshop preparation. I went home, repacked my duffel bag, and headed back to Reagan Airport.

It was the same airport where I had landed a few hours earlier, but it was a different me. Suddenly I was alone in the universe. Everyone else in the building, so it seemed to me, from the Delta Airlines counter attendant to the Starbucks barista, had a stable job and secure future laid out for them. My khaki dress slacks and navy blazer disguised the fact that I was nobody, unwanted by my organization and with an uncertain future. That evening I called Lonnie and gave her the news. She empathized, since she had felt the emotional toll that the past two years had taken on me. But she was also the person in our marriage who paid the bills, and the prospect of a mortgage and car payment and no dependable income was a scary thing. True to form, her response was, "Okay, we'll figure it out. I love you." On her own, however, she shed plenty of tears.

I gave my talk at Carson-Newman, neglecting to work the topic of my pending termination into the presentation, and returned to Washington, where over the next few days I informed other family members about this unexpected development. Rich Gathro, a former vice president of the CCCU with a pastor's heart, had learned the news and happened to be in town. He visited me in my office and read to me Psalm 34. Anna sent me a passage from Henri Nouwen that I have referred to time and again:

> Just imagine what Mary was saying in the words, "I am the handmaiden of the Lord. Let what you have said be done to me." She was saying, "I don't know what all this means, but I trust that good things will happen." She trusted so deeply that her waiting was open to all possibilities. And she did not want to control them.

She knew that when she listened carefully, she could trust what was going to happen.

To wait open-endedly is an enormously radical attitude toward life. So is to trust that something will happen to us that is far beyond our own imaginings. So, too, is giving up control over our future and letting God define our life, trusting that God molds us according to his love and not according to our fear.[16]

I was scheduled to stay in Washington over the following weekend, so I had several days to put things in order and pack up my office. I also would be returning periodically over the next few months, so there was no need yet for final farewells, but boxing up one's books and belongings and loading them into a rental car does give one a sense of finality. I have always enjoyed long solitary car trips, and this one in particular gave me plenty of opportunity to ponder, in Nouwen's words, "what all this means" and whether "good things" might come of it. And I had plenty of pondering to do; I was a middle-aged academic looking for a new career. I wasn't tossed completely overboard, but I was in a leaky raft floating away from the mother ship on a vast ocean, and I needed to start paddling to an island of refuge before the raft sank. As it turned out, that refuge would come from an unlikely source, and demonstrate once again that God has a sense of humor.

ooooo

LANDSCAPING INTERLUDE

And so it was that on a brisk, sunny Michigan morning in September, one week after returning from Washington, DC, I found myself shoveling topsoil into a wheelbarrow for seventeen dollars an hour. A few months earlier, our neighbors had some landscaping work done, and Lonnie and I struck up a conversation with the worker. Mark ran a landscaping business and worked alone because finding responsible laborers was difficult. He remarked at the time, "If you ever want some work to do, just let me know."

I wasn't planning a career change to landscaping, but I had always enjoyed manual labor, and my CCCU work was now part time. Since I was still in the process of figuring out next steps, spending a few days a week with Mark seemed like a good idea. Besides, with our financial future unclear, generating some additional cash flow made sense. Lonnie, a Pennsylvania farm girl who wasn't afraid of hard work, had joined Mark's payroll two weeks earlier. We worked together one particularly warm day, chopping and hauling away large stalks of fountain grass in the hot sun. While I enjoyed working with her, seeing your wife, a professional pianist, doing manual labor with gloves on to protect her valuable fingers because your professional future is in doubt isn't exactly an ego-booster.

For the next two months, until the early winter snows came to West Michigan, I landscaped two or three days a week—pruning bushes, spreading topsoil to seed new lawns, mowing grass, and raking leaves. September and October are some of the best weather months in Michigan, and Mark and I would typically begin the day with three layers of clothing and be down to one by afternoon.

133

A pair of heavy cotton slacks had served as my Friday casual pants. Now they became my work pants and would dangle from a hook above the basement stairs between workdays, the dried mud on the knees making them hang unnaturally stiff. My Merrill trail runners made for sturdy, comfortable work shoes.

Not much planting occurs in the fall, so most of our work was maintenance, and that became increasingly true as the majestic oak and maple trees in East Grand Rapids began dropping their leaves. I learned to rake leaves like a professional. Old-fashioned fan-shaped flexible metal rakes are far superior to those large clunky plastic monstrosities one finds in the aisles of Home Depot. Their wider intervals scratch cleanly through the grass and leave the smaller plant material to decompose and nourish the soil. Mark showed me how, when the metal tongs clog up with leaves, you rotate the handle 180 degrees, swipe once on the ground, and they magically disappear. True to my "reformer" nature, I developed a more efficient way to haul leaves on tarps by threading a rope through the eyelets on one end, thereby enabling me to walk forward with the rope around my waist rather than shuffle backward. I especially liked pulling up old summer flowers by hand from plant beds, where, on all fours, I felt close to the earth. The Celtic prayer that had described my painting and study routine in graduate school came back to mind:

> Labor and rest, work and ease; the busy hand,
> and then the skilled thought:
> This blending of opposites is the secret of the joy
> of living.

Unfortunately, while Mark liked to do much of his work by hand, he also needed to turn a profit. As the leaves began falling in earnest in late October, therefore, gas-powered backpack leaf blowers occupied a greater proportion of our time. While I did appreciate the efficiency of the device—and was amazed by Mark's dexterity with it—having a small engine revving a foot below your eardrums is probably not what the Celtic monks had in mind when they described the virtues of manual labor.

When the leaf blowers were silent, Mark would often enlighten me on the benefits of Donald Trump's presidency. But he was also sensitive to my work situation and to others' perceptions. A couple of his clients were my nearby neighbors, but recognizing the potential awkwardness, he never asked me to help him with their lawns. Indeed, in modern society, when one moves from an executive position to mowing lawns, one appreciates the extent to which our identities stem from our work. It was about this time that I read Amor Towles's novel *A Gentleman in Moscow*, about a Russian nobleman who runs afoul of the Communist Party and is exiled to a hotel for the rest of his life and works there as a waiter. Towles's words resonated with me:

> Like the Freemasons, the Confederacy of the Humbled is a close-knit brotherhood whose members travel with no outward markings, but who know each other at a glance. For having fallen suddenly from grace, those in the Confederacy share a certain perspective. Knowing beauty, influence, fame, and privilege to be borrowed rather than bestowed, they are not easily impressed. They remain committed to living among their peers, but they greet adulation with caution, ambition with sympathy, and condescension with an inward smile.[17]

Often while landscaping, I didn't necessarily feel inferior, just invisible. Towles writes of his protagonist, "having lived his life in the heat of battle, at the crux of conversation, and in the twentieth row with its privileged view—that is, in the very thick of things—suddenly he finds himself invisible to friend and foe alike." I now understood that feeling of invisibility. Homeowners who formerly I might have shared a table with at an Amway Grand fund-raiser, or who might have attended a banquet that I hosted at Cornerstone, now seemed to inhabit a different world from me. Once when Mark and I were working at a house, the owner came out to talk, and Mark introduced me to him by name. I continued my work, and at the end of their ten-minute conversation, the home-owner casually remarked, "Bye, Rick." I was astounded that he recalled my name, and afterward, whenever I ran or biked past the house, I would silently bless the owner (whose name, ironically, I don't remember).

Of course, not planning to be a waiter in my particular restaurant forever, during my nonlandscaping days I was also applying for academic positions. But the wheels of academia grind slowly. Along with humility, therefore, I had plenty of time that fall to learn patience, which is a trait that has never really suited me. I've only had one type of recurring nightmare in life: it's not snakes or falling; rather, I need to get somewhere quickly but some-how can't do so. Typically these dreams are set in airports, where my plane is departing and all sorts of absurd events happen to prevent me from reaching the gate. Or I'm in a bike race and need to change a flat tire, and the next thing I know, I'm reassembling the entire front fork while the peloton speeds away. Clearly I have issues with waiting and not being in control of my situation.

I was reading a new genre of books, courtesy of some of my friends, that spoke to these issues. As Henri Nou-wen observed, "Sometimes we have no choice but to let other people, circumstances, or events determine our life direction." Unable to wave a magic wand and change my situation, I sought—imperfectly at best—to enter a season of "active waiting." As Nouwen wrote: "Active waiting is essential to the spiritual life. Whenever there is lack of clarity, it's time to wait. But the paradox is that waiting requires full attention to the present moment."[18] I sought to appreciate what it means to fully live in each day without mulling over the past or speculating about the future—what my daughter Anna would call dwelling in "This, Here, Now." I wrote to a friend toward the end of my landscaping season,

> Each morning, I take mental stock and realize that I have enough food and drink for the day and the house is heated and dry. And I have the best wife in the world and four healthy kids, all of whom have college degrees and none of whom are in jail. So this day is all set, and the next one is God's responsibility, not mine. Then I tell myself the words that Andrew Brunson, a pastor who spent two years in a Turkish prison, recited each day—"God loves me. He's true. He's faithful. He has not abandoned me"—and I get on with my routine.

My pastor and spiritual guide, Rob Peterson, recommended Richard Rohr's *Falling Upward: A Spirituality for the Two Halves of Life.* The first half of life, Rohr writes, consists of struggle, achievement, and acquiring influence. The second half is "a much deeper river, hidden beneath the appearances," that transcends but also includes the earlier half. But to truly arrive at the deeper life, Rohr says, some kind of falling or failing must be experienced. He writes, "We must stumble and fall, I'm sorry to say. And that does not mean reading about it. We must actually be out of the driver's seat for a while or we will never learn how to give up control to the Real Guide." Rohr concludes, "In the end, we do not so much reclaim what we have lost as discover a significantly new self in and through the process."[19]

Being out of the driver's seat, however, doesn't mean passivity; it just means that we resist the urge to grab the steering wheel. Amid my landscaping work and waiting for the next thing, I resorted, as usual, to road biking to understand my situation. Cyclists have different cadences, or rates at which they pedal the bike. Large riders with strong legs often grind away in a high gear at low rpms; skinny guys like me like to spin away at a high cadence. The key is to find the cadence you're comfortable with, keep your butt in the saddle, and keep pedaling. Sometimes when you're going uphill or into a stiff wind, you pedal like crazy but don't feel like you're getting anywhere. Other times, on a downslope or with a tailwind, you feel like you're flying. The effort doesn't change, just the results. That autumn, I continued to work ten hours a day as usual, sometimes for the CCCU, sometimes on landscaping, sometimes on job applications, sometimes just reading and writing, hoping that "new things" would eventually come.

Several years ago, in the Tour de France, one of the riders was clipped by a camera vehicle and went soaring off the road into a barbed-wire fence (it makes for a spectacular YouTube clip). He responded like any bike racer would—he got up, unleashed a mouthful of expletives, picked the barbed wire out of his skin, hopped on a replacement bike, and finished the 120-mile stage. There have been times in life when I've pictured myself as the biker who crashed into barbed wire. What I might lack in intelligence or eloquence I make up for in stubbornness, and in those times the only thing I can do is get back on the bike, keep my cadence high, and trust that God will bring about good things someday.

Sure enough, despite my fears that I would be the only former provost to earn a living mowing lawns, eventually I returned to full-time academic work. We didn't have to sell our house, and our income has been more than sufficient for our needs. In retrospect, it would be nice to think that my time "out of the driver's seat" working as a landscaper created a transformed, serene, more powerful version of myself, kind of like Luke Skywalker emerging from Yoda's swamp as a fully trained Jedi knight. Hopefully some difference came about, but if so, it's clearly just one of degree, not of kind. As Lonnie can attest, I still quickly become unhinged if I choose the slower checkout line at the grocery store or get stuck behind a slow driver on a two-lane road.

I also noticed, however, during my months of landscaping, that gradually, imperceptibly, my hands came to resemble a laborer's hands. They developed callouses and a toughness not through any intentional effort on my part but as a by-product of long hours working a shovel or a rake. And perhaps over time, my soul also developed some new qualities without me noticing. My landscaping interlude didn't transform me into a new person, but hopefully it helped me to identify a little more with the Confederacy of the Humbled and to be more grateful for God's provision. At Cornerstone University, my post-lunch walking circuit that took me by classes and faculty offices had served as my reminder of God's blessings on the institution. Now when I went running in East Grand Rapids, I developed a route that took me by the houses whose lawns I had mowed and leaves I had raked. Anytime I needed a reminder of God's faithfulness and provision, the neighborhood run was the perfect solution. I would need more reminders over the next few years.

∞∞∞

SEVEN

Back in Business

ONE CAN PICTURE higher education as a collection of concentric circles. The innermost circle, where the core activities of teaching and learning take place, is the classroom, and a slightly larger circle around that includes other venues such as laboratories and the library. The next circle consists of midlevel administrators such as deans, chairs, and student support staff, who help to decide what students should learn and how, and seek to foster an environment where good learning happens. Then there's the circle of senior academic administrators and presidents, who hire and manage the people doing the core work, set budgets, raise money, and represent their particular institution to the broader world. Next, there's the world of higher education associations, such as the CCCU, that support, equip, and advocate for institutions collectively. Finally, there's an outer circle of for-profit consultants, businesses, marketing firms, and tech companies that provide services to colleges and universities. One irony of the higher education ecosystem is that, generally speaking, the further one moves from the center to the periphery of higher education, the more lucrative the enterprise.

As I prepared to leave the CCCU and explored options, eventually I found myself inhabiting the outer circle of for-profit educational support businesses. In fact, one simple indicator of my professional journey is the evolution of my email address from dot-edu to dot-org to dot-com. Decades earlier, during my year at

TelWatch, I had concluded that the business world wasn't for me. Now, to my surprise, I returned to that world through the back door of academic consulting.

ooooo

If shifting from a desk job to landscaping required some getting used to, so too did the days in Grand Rapids when I wasn't landscaping. My typical day would begin at 7:00 a.m. with a cup of coffee and devotions on the red sofa in the living room, set by a window overlooking Argentina Drive. That way I could watch busy people speeding off to work and parents walking their children to the local elementary school in our Mayberry-like neighborhood. Our cat, Muffin (it's a long story), returning from his nightly activities, would be waiting for me at the front door, sometimes leaving the bottom half of a mouse on the doorstep as a souvenir. He would hop up beside me on the sofa for a chin rub, unless Lonnie—the preferred option—was sitting across the room in the brown leather recliner. Then after a visit to the food dish, he would saunter up the stairs to the master bedroom to sleep the day away.

By October, Lonnie's dance card as a pianist had filled up and her time as landscaping queen was over, so she would head off to a local university or the Grand Rapids Ballet. The Kawai shared the living room with me; we were both a bit worse for wear after a couple of decades of moving around. I don't play piano, so it generally sat unused until Lonnie returned from work. After a half hour, it was time for me and my second cup of coffee to head upstairs to work in the spare bedroom, which was now my home office.

But to do what? How does one go about forging a new role in higher education? In my case, through trial and error. When I biked in Washington, DC, my philosophy was to never clip out of the pedals, which required remaining in constant motion. That can be difficult to do in Washington traffic. Thus, while I would get a vigorous workout, the particular route I took depended on the traffic lights and other traffic patterns that I encountered. If the light was green, I kept going straight; if it was yellow, I went straight faster. If it turned red, I generally turned right, maintained my speed, and adjusted my ride accordingly. Now I applied the same method to professional opportunities: wherever a light was green, I kept moving forward; if a light turned red, then it was time to veer in a different direction.

I still had part-time work with the CCCU, overseeing research and scholarship, and I continued my routine of periodically emailing chief academic officers. And of course, I applied for several university jobs, primarily dean and provost positions, many of which are posted in the early fall. I was still relatively young, had a decent record of accomplishments, and was well known throughout the CCCU. The reality, however, is that Christian colleges and universities need to diversify their leadership structures. Diversity among students has increased significantly over the past two decades, but the faculty and administrative ranks lag behind. Thus, academic institutions generally are making a concerted effort to hire females and leaders of color. Of course, plenty of white males still land academic leadership positions. But for such candidates, it helps to bring something noteworthy to the table, such as a record of launching innovative new programs or significant experience working in diverse settings.

I wasn't sure I displayed any such notable qualities. Moreover, academic search processes tend to proceed at a glacial pace. So rather than putting all of my eggs in that basket, it made sense to explore other options as well. I applied to organizations such as the Nagel Institute for World Christianity, a local nonprofit dedicated to increasing biblical literacy, and the group that I had worked with while a provost at Cornerstone, the Colossian Forum. In each case, there was some level of interest on both sides, but while I could try to motivate myself to be passionate about those enterprises, it was clearly an effort. Both parties concluded that it wasn't a perfect fit.

Thus, I arrived where many former academic administrators end up: consulting. As a provost at Cornerstone, I had been skeptical about the idea of spending money on outside consultants when so many more immediate needs seemed to merit funding. In fact, during the budget cuts in my first year, one of the first items to go was our contract with an educational research firm. But for colleges and universities, especially small ones, hiring consultants can be a wise decision. As a homeowner, it doesn't make sense for me to take a plumbing course and buy expensive tools to fix the occasional plumbing problem that may arise in my house. I'm better off hiring a plumber when I need one. So, too, there are a number of functions at academic institutions that are better outsourced to experts. Universities are complicated institutions, and no one person has all the answers on how to run them well. Moreover, higher education is a competitive business, and $30,000 spent on a consultant whose insights give you an advantage over the competition may be money well spent.

Because most private institutions are tuition-dependent, some of the biggest consulting firms in higher education focus on marketing and enrollment. Ruffalo Noel Levitz, for example, will review your operations, expand your applicant funnel, and hopefully get you more students—for a hefty price. A subspecies of the enrollment consultant is the online program manager, or OPM. These companies cater to colleges and universities that want to expand into the online education market but either don't have the resources and expertise to do so themselves, or they have faculty who hold their noses at online education and want to stay as far away from it as possible. In the latter case, hiring an outside firm to make the sausage at least means that less of the odor wafts toward the faculty building. OPMs tend to be viewed with skepticism by academic traditionalists, both because they specialize in a segment of education that purists tend to perceive as less rigorous, and because they typically get paid by taking a significant portion of the per-student enrollment revenue. Enroll a new student, and 60 percent of the tuition goes to you, 40 percent goes to the OPM.

In academic affairs specifically, several areas can benefit from consultants. One common function to outsource is institutional research, which can be difficult for a small institution to do well in-house. Organizations such as the Education Advisory Board provide valuable services to hundreds of colleges and universities by researching market opportunities, uncovering underlying threats, and surveying best practices. Then there are a host of independent consultants—often former college presidents, vice presidents for enrollment, or chief academic officers who picked up some useful experiences in their previous role that would benefit another institution. For example, Robert Andringa, former president of the CCCU, serves as a specialist in board relations and board development, helping to improve an area of private higher education that is often a weakness.

As I pedaled the higher-education landscape looking for green lights in fall 2018, academic consulting emerged as a real interest. Having spent the past three years interacting with over a hundred chief academic officers, I certainly had connections. But what did I have that might be of value? Strategic planning is a fruitful area for consultants, but I've never been strongly interested in that area. You spend a year planning out the next decade of your institution, then COVID-19 hits and much of the plan is obsolete. Accreditation is another fruitful area for consultants. The accreditation process is daunting, and the stakes are high, so academics who have experience in this area can be valuable. Accreditation, however, generally appeals to individuals on the wonky, more detail-minded end of the administrative spectrum. My eyes tend to glaze over when I encounter terms such as "program learning outcomes," "comprehensive assessment strategies," or "closing the loop" to achieve "continuous quality improvement."

What I did have, as a former dean, provost, and CCCU vice president, was an assortment of skills that, cobbled together, might make for a successful enterprise. So I explored some possibilities and reached out to contacts. One of the first was an old friend, Phil Payne, who operated a successful study-abroad program in Quito, Ecuador. I had helped him refine the program when I was a dean at John Brown University and had sent students there while at Cornerstone. Having an experienced academic who could review his programs and help him connect with more colleges was certainly of interest to Phil, and we discussed the possibility of an ongoing relationship.

Also, from my experiences at John Brown and Cornerstone, I have always enjoyed working in faculty-administration relations. Professors on many campuses are discontent due to financial stresses, high teaching loads, and the contrarian disposition of the typical faculty member. This was an area where I thought I could contribute something of value. In October, I reached out to Laurie Schreiner, a professor at Azusa Pacific University who was developing a faculty-thriving survey, and we teamed up to pilot the project at a few schools and hopefully expand it in the future. Moreover, I had a knack for identifying inefficiencies and streamlining processes—my biker's obsession with efficiency at work—and had experience working in a variety of institutional structures that could be useful to others. Finally, my personal experience in multiple academic roles could be beneficial to provosts seeking to mentor new or aspiring academics in their own institutions.

In November, therefore, I started an LLC creatively entitled Ostrander Academic Consulting. I played with a biking theme for the name and logo, which fortunately Lonnie vetoed. I reached out to my network of provosts toward the end of the fall semester; not surprisingly, I only had a few bites. Two provost friends had deans whom they wanted to develop into senior leaders, and they asked me to mentor those individuals. As Christmas approached, I had my limited CCCU work, a couple of clients for coaching, several job applications pending, and a website—hardly a thriving consulting enterprise. Then on Christmas Eve, I received an email from the provost of a university in California. He was considering restructuring academic operations and requested my assistance in reviewing the current structure and proposing changes. It wasn't much, but it was a real consulting project that included a trip to the West Coast in January, and it enabled me to go into the Christmas holidays with at least some hope for the future.

ooooo

The first week of January, in what seemed to be an unrelated event at the time, I visited Israel. A few months earlier, a representative of an organization called Passages had reached out to me in my role as a CCCU vice president. Passages is a Christian organization that takes US college students on ten-day immersive trips to Israel.

The purpose is both spiritual and political: while Passages seeks to deepen students' Christian faith through exposure to the Holy Land, it also exists to foster a more positive view of Israel among young Americans. To expand their orbit, Passages was inviting leaders of Christian organizations on an all-expenses-paid trip to Israel. I had never been there, saw a lot of empty spaces in my January calendar, and accepted their invitation.

Because of Passages' pro-Israel orientation, I was prepared for a certain level of bias and highly orchestrated visits to idyllic Israeli settings. And while the portrayal of Israel was generally positive, I was impressed with the operational efficiency of the organization and Passages' willingness to expose students to multiple perspectives, including a session with a passionately anti-Israel Palestinian nationalist. I concluded that Christian college students would benefit from the Passages experience, and because the cost was highly subsidized, the trip was accessible to a broader cross section of students than the typical short-term study-abroad program. Passages was unknown to most Christian colleges, so during the trip I discussed with the organization's leaders how I could help them develop partnerships within the CCCU.

The first such opportunity was the annual CCCU Presidents' Conference, scheduled to take place just a few weeks later in Washington, DC. I reached out to some contacts, and we arranged a dinner for several presidents and spouses with Passages leadership at one of Washington's best restaurants. In my role overseeing research at the CCCU, I was also scheduled to present an award at the conference's opening banquet. A polar vortex hit the United States the week of the conference. My original flight to Washington was canceled, then a second flight. Carving out a new living as a consultant, I was not about to let a gathering of over a hundred college presidents slip away. I woke up at 3:00 a.m. on the morning of the event, rented a car at the Grand Rapids airport, and headed east. For the first hour, I struggled to see the road through swirling lake-effect snow, but once I cleared Lansing, a northwest gale basically pushed me 650 miles to Washington. I arrived in time for a nap and shower before the banquet. Shirley Hoogstra mentioned to the gathered presidents that I drove there from Grand Rapids, which either impressed them with my devotion to duty or convinced them that I was crazy.

The following evening, we hosted the Passages dinner with CCCU presidents, and it dawned on me: my network *was* my best asset. I had always enjoyed bringing different people and organizations together. Moreover, I understood Christian colleges, cared about their success, and would not recommend an opportunity or partnership that I didn't feel was in their best interests. Thus, Passages became a long-term client, and collaboration between organizations became a key part of my consulting work. I had cultivated a reputation over the years as the guy who knew people and who could make connections. Doing so was not just good for others but could be good for me as well.

By February, therefore, I had a collection of small projects such as the faculty-thriving initiative, Passages, coaching deans, and a few other prospects on the horizon. I could tie some barrels together to make a raft, but it wasn't something I'd want to paddle out on the open sea. Fortunately, there was one more barrel out there.

ooooo

Two years earlier, while a CCCU vice president, I received an email from a provost requesting the CCCU's assistance in forming what he called an "online course-sharing consortium." He also referred me to a company called Acadeum that could help us do it. So far in my career, my main contribution to online education had been writing an article for *Books and Culture* questioning the value of digital learning, but I was willing to consider the possibility. At first, I had no idea what they were talking about, but eventually I realized that the "online" rhetoric was throwing me off, and the "consortium" was the important part.

In academics, a consortium is a group of schools that agree to offer classes collaboratively in order to operate more efficiently. If College X typically teaches Business Statistics to fifteen students, and ten miles away College Y teaches the same course to ten students, why not just combine the classes into one? Some institutional friction must be resolved, such as the transfer of credits and the belief by professors at both institutions that "No one teaches Business Stats as well as we teach Business Stats." But if one can work through the obstacles, course sharing can help colleges and universities operate more efficiently and provide students with a greater variety of course options. For example, since 1965, five institutions in Amherst, Massachusetts, have operated the "Five Colleges Consortium." A bus shuttles students from one institution to classes at partner institutions.

The limits of such an arrangement, of course, are that only schools in close proximity can share courses. What the founders of Acadeum realized, however, was that online education opens up vast possibilities for course sharing. No longer are collaborating institutions limited by geography or the need to align class schedules. They just need a means to communicate with each other to identify courses to share, then move student data and payments efficiently between the institutions. Acadeum created a Web-based platform to do that. Gradually, I figured out that Acadeum wasn't an OPM; they weren't building and selling online courses, they were essentially functioning as Airbnb for private higher education. The teaching institution is a homeowner with an empty bedroom (or in this case a "seat" in an online course) and would like to gain some revenue from it. The home institution is a traveler in search of a room, or in this case a seat in a course to provide to its student. Just as Airbnb facilitates the partnership between homeowners and travelers, Acadeum does the same for institutions.

Once I grasped the concept, it was obvious that the CCCU was a perfect arena for such a course-sharing network, which functions best when participating institutions have a high level of mutual trust and mission alignment. At CCCU's 2018 International Forum on Christian Higher Education in Dallas, therefore, eight institutions met and formed the CCCU Online Course-Sharing Consortium. Growth was slow initially, but as more institutions grasped the concept, the initiative gained momentum, and growing the consortium became a significant part of my work at the CCCU.

Soon other networks of colleges were adopting the Acadeum platform for course sharing. In fall 2018, the CIC also launched an online consortium on the Acadeum platform. With over seven hundred members, the CIC had the potential to become a much larger course-sharing network. To grow such networks, Acadeum needed spokespersons who spoke the language of academics—not technology or business—and who had the trust of chief academic officers for whom "online course sharing" was a foreign concept. When one of Acadeum's cofounders learned that I was leaving the CCCU, he asked if I would be interested in a part-time relationship with the company.

In February 2019, therefore, adding Acadeum to my other activities made a career in independent consulting a legitimate possibility. The same month, however, two provost searches that I was involved in culminated in campus visits for Lonnie and me. Both institutions were quality Christian universities with intriguing prospects. I now faced a different challenge from that of four months earlier: discerning the best course from among some attractive possibilities.

Toward the end of the month, I had my final CCCU conference in St. Petersburg, Florida. After the conference, Lonnie and I spent two days with former CCCU vice president Rich Gathro and his wife, Kathy, in their Florida condominium. I had one provost offer on the table and another one likely on the way. Such positions offered significant attractions—not just the opportunity to be in a Christian college again, but also financial stability and, to be honest, the status that comes from occupying a leadership role. Independent consulting entailed risk, no doubt, but also the excitement of doing a variety of new things and the challenge of having to hustle to ensure that the next job was on the horizon. Whenever I have a choice between roads, whether in biking or in life, an annoying little voice in my head tells me to take the steeper one. As we discussed the options with the Gathros on their balcony, Kathy asked, "Of the options, which one gets you most excited?" It was a simple question with a clear answer. I called both college presidents to withdraw from consideration and jumped into the consulting boat.

ooooo

My time with the CCCU officially ended in May. I had ongoing contracts with Acadeum and Passages and queries out for some other projects. We had taken the risk on consulting, but finances were a legitimate question, especially during the upcoming summer months, when colleges and universities generally go into vacation mode. Fortunately, a month earlier I had run into our next-door neighbor at the local Starbucks. After the usual small talk, he said, "I have a strange question for you: Would you be interested in renting out your house for six weeks this summer?" He went on to explain that he had arranged with a local family to rent them his house while theirs was being remodeled. Then he ended up selling his house unexpectedly and now faced the unenviable task of informing the family that his house was no longer available. He wondered if perhaps we might be able to bail him out.

"For how much?" I asked.

"$10,000."

"I think we can make that happen."

Lonnie agreed, but that raised the obvious question, where would we live for the summer? We sent out some queries to friends in the area, and among the replies was an email from George Marsden, who lived a mile from us in Grand Rapids. "Lucie and I are at our lake cottage all summer," he replied. "You're welcome to stay in our house."

Thus, my consulting career officially launched that summer out of my former mentor's home office. I occupied, literally, the prestigious George Marsden chair of academic consulting. In late June, I traveled to Austin for an Acadeum company gathering and experienced a new world of tech start-ups: the office was on the fourth floor of a WeWork building, complete with kombucha and lager on tap. I was one of the few fifty-plus persons in the building; my tucked-in shirt and clean-shaven face clearly outed me as an academic nerd crashing the Austin creative scene.

Two weeks later, I traveled to Israel with Passages, accompanying a group of forty Samford University students, in order to learn the program better and to recommend changes. Returning home, I had my first Acadeum Zoom call with Mount St. Joseph University, a small Catholic institution in Ohio. My computer's calendar bungled the meeting time, and ten minutes after it was scheduled to begin, I received a call on my cell phone from the registrar, who had assembled the director of institutional technology, chief financial officer, and academic dean for the meeting. Unable to get my Zoom to work, I conducted the meeting by phone. The questions from the IT director might as well have been in Sanskrit from what I understood of them. Amazingly, the university joined the CIC Consortium, which I can only attribute to beginner's luck or divine intervention, or both.

As the academic year began, I became something of a Swiss army knife of consultants. My friend Mark Sargent, provost at Westmont College, invited me to speak at the college's annual faculty retreat on higher-education trends. The Faculty Thriving Project garnered a couple of campus invitations. I flew to California to meet with Phil Payne and his assistant for a day of brainstorming. Phil Payne's study-abroad enterprise was expanding, and I agreed to advise him on academics and introduce his program to more colleges and universities. The Templeton Religion Trust hired me to conduct a study on attitudes toward science and religion at ten leading Christian colleges and universities. I gave a series of talks at Crown College in Minnesota. In November, I represented Acadeum at the annual CIC chief academic officers' conference. After attending countless conferences as an administrator, it was strange being the guy on the other side of the sponsor's table, offering free swag to entice passersby into conversations about how online course-sharing could transform their institution. In all, between regular clients and stand-alone projects, I had steady work and enjoyed the rhythm of travel and working at home. When contacted about academic leadership positions, I engaged with those that seemed most attractive but otherwise focused on the business of academic consulting.

In fact, January and February 2020 were about as good as it gets for an independent consultant. In late January I visited Madison, Wisconsin, to explore Christian study-abroad opportunities for students at the University of Wisconsin. While there I visited a local Acadeum client, Elmwood College. From there I flew to Washington, DC, for the annual CCCU Presidents' Conference.

After a week at home, I flew to San Diego to represent Acadeum at the CCCU Multi-Academic Conference. A week after returning from San Diego, February culminated in a weeklong trip to Rome for Lonnie and me. Phil Payne was partnering with a study-abroad program there, and he wanted my help in reviewing the program and making recommendations. Lonnie and I flew in a few days early to explore Rome on our own, then joined Phil for four days with the study program.

Early that week, Italian news outlets began carrying stories of a "COVID-19" virus that had made its way from China to northern Italy. Cities in the north such as Milan, Bologna, and Venice began taking precautions. By the end of the week, northern Italy was shutting down and masks were appearing more frequently on Rome buses and subways. On Saturday morning, as Lonnie and I prepared to leave for Leonardo Da Vinci Airport, the students in the study program received word from their university that they were being brought home. We arrived back in the United States on March 1, and soon the entire world, it seemed, was shutting down.

ooooo

So what does an academic consultant do during a pandemic? In my case, not much. Visiting campuses was no longer an option, and colleges and universities shifted their focus to riding out the pandemic. Study-abroad programs scrambled to send their students home, close up shop, then wait and see what was left once the pandemic subsided. Our daughter Anna was working as a staff member for the CCCU's Uganda Studies Program at the time. She and the other staff took a few dozen students to Entebbe airport, then spent a few days closing up the program. On a Sunday evening, she boarded one of the last planes out of Entebbe, a few hours before Uganda shut down completely. For the next several months, Anna lived in our basement, Lonnie taught piano lessons by Zoom, and I worked in the upstairs bedroom.

A pandemic was bad for independent consultants but good for Acadeum. Online education was now the only game in town, and as colleges and universities scrambled to provide enough online courses for the coming fall semester, filling in gaps with courses from other institutions became a common strategy. I had demonstrated my value to the organization over the past several months, and Acadeum wanted me to join the company full time. During a global pandemic, having a full-time employer seemed like a good idea. Thus, in April 2020, I became "vice president for academic partnerships" at Acadeum, which is a fancy title for an academic salesperson.

To my surprise, I excelled at sales despite my introverted nature and academic traditionalism. "Sales" is not a popular term among academics; in fact, one easy way to annoy a professor is to refer to students as "customers." Over the years, however, I had come to realize that in one way or another, just about everyone in academics is also a salesperson. The professor who needs to recruit one more student in her feminist literature course for it to avoid the provost's chopping block is doing sales. So is the professor who needs to persuade ten students to participate in a summer study-program trip to Paris, or the philosopher seeking to entice freshmen from his Introduction to Philosophy course to become philosophy majors so the program escapes the scrutiny of the CFO. And so too, of course, is the college president trying to land a ten-million-dollar lead gift to launch a science building campaign. At the CCCU, we were selling as well. We sold our conferences to attendees; I was selling our study-abroad programs to administrators at member schools. We may use different terms to describe it, but sales is central to higher education.

At Acadeum, I embraced the role of salesperson. This was my green light to pedal through, so I kept my cadence high. My work at the CCCU had prepared me for the annoying necessity of sending multiple emails before receiving a response. I was no longer a provost, and emails from outside parties tend to sink to the bottom of an administrator's unanswered emails inbox. Being persistent didn't bother me because I believed in what we had to offer. For private colleges and universities, cooperation is a key to survival in a challenging future, and the sooner they realize that fact, the better. Furthermore, since the Acadeum system took a while for me to grasp,

I became adept at explaining it well to other academics, employing Airbnb, Google Maps, and Keurigs as useful analogies. Finally, sales fit my intense road-biker mentality. As the signed contracts increased, I enjoyed the sense of achievement that came with them.

Throughout the pandemic, therefore, I had the good fortune of a stable, well-paying job doing work that I believed was good for higher education. Despite misgivings and frequent doubts, God had led me through my landscaping interlude to an interesting new profession. Deep in my soul, however, formed at Moody, Michigan, and Notre Dame, was a love for academics and working in the daily grind of teaching and administration. As much as we liked our community in Grand Rapids, Lonnie and I missed being members of the unique subcultures that are academic communities. We sensed that working at a college might still be in our future, if the right one came along.

In the fall of 2020, Mark Sargent announced his retirement as provost from Westmont College and I was nominated for the position. I had progressed enough in my career to be discriminating about professional opportunities, but Westmont, the site of my first CCCU experience as a young professor in 1998, checked all the right boxes. A residential, undergraduate-focused liberal arts college, it excelled in the type of education that resonated with Lonnie and me. It employed quality professors who were committed to teaching, scholarship, and student mentoring. As one of the most academically rigorous CCCU institutions, it attracted bright students who were serious about learning. Westmont also happened to be located in Santa Barbara, California. While such a beautiful location might have been a significant draw to some, a Midwesterner like myself actually prefers the greenery and the seasons of Michigan. If you're going to leave Michigan, however, there are worse places to end up than Santa Barbara, especially if you're into road biking. It helped that our oldest son, Ryan, and his wife, Hannah, lived in downtown Santa Barbara.

As it turned out, Westmont's provost position did not materialize for me. The interview process, however, brought us into the Westmont orbit, and in the summer of 2021, the college created a new role that closely matched my gifts and interests. I was offered a position as assistant to the president for academic innovation and director of Westmont's new downtown campus. Also, Lonnie was offered a part-time position in the Music Department, which confirmed the decision for us. We sold the little white house on Argentina Drive and prepared to move to California.

∞∞∞

How does a traditional academic, formed by a Bible college, the University of Michigan, and the University of Notre Dame, make sense of two years in the dot-com educational world? First, I was genuinely impressed with the desire of for-profits to benefit higher education, and their level of competence in doing so. Companies such as Acadeum, for example, cast a wide net for candidates and pay good salaries, and as a result, they hire talented people. As I often remarked to my fellow Christian academics, "Acadeum just has a lot of really smart people working there."

At the same time, I experienced firsthand the fundamental difference between a dot-com and a dot-edu. "For-profit" really means what it says. A college serves its mission, as stewarded by a board of trustees, which hires the president and seeks to preserve and sustain that mission. For-profits serve a different master. As an independent for-profit consultant, I served my wife, who paid the bills at the end of the month. Acadeum is accountable to its investors, who expect to see evidence of growing profitability. While I took satisfaction in Acadeum's rapid growth—and still enjoy working with the company on a part-time basis—when the agenda of weekly Zoom meetings moved to quotas and Key Performance Indicators, my eyes tended to glaze over and I was reminded that I was still hardwired as a traditional academic. In the case of the best for-profits, such as Acadeum, their success is closely aligned with the success of their clients. Nevertheless, the client, whether a university or a company, is a means to an end—becoming profitable—not an end in itself. The bird perched on the back of the rhinoceros eating insects is doing a service for the rhinoceros; but ultimately, the bird is there for the bugs, not the rhino.

And so Lonnie and I headed off to California to rejoin an academic institution. Sadly, the Kawai didn't join us. We concluded that it had endured enough cross-country trips and was better off staying in Grand Rapids. Lonnie taught piano lessons to the daughter of two ballet instructors, and we sold the Kawai to them for a hundred dollars. Muffin, too, remained in West Michigan. He upgraded to a house of four male college students at Grand Valley State University and became an Instagram celebrity. Minus one piano and one cat, we headed west in our Honda CRV. My circuitous academic career seemed to be culminating at one of America's premier Christian liberal arts colleges.

MOUNTAIN INTERLUDE

On a bright Sunday morning in August 2021, Lonnie and I drove west out of Las Vegas in our white Honda CRV loaded with valuables that we were reluctant to trust to a moving van. It was the final day of our cross-country trek from Grand Rapids to Santa Barbara. The sun rose behind us as we were greeted by a "Welcome to California" billboard along the highway. Spotify played "Build My Life," one of the songs that had gotten us through the past three years, with the chorus, "I will build my life upon Your love, it is a firm foundation." We had passed through three years of uncertainty and finally arrived at a new and fulfilling place.

There's an iconic cycling climb in the mountains overlooking Santa Barbara called Gibraltar Road. It starts just above the city and climbs nearly four thousand feet in less than ten miles. About three-quarters of the way up, there's a dip in the road, and if you're new to the climb, you conclude that the climb is almost over, and your body begins to relax. Then the road curves to the left and slaps you in the face with the steepest section yet, made even more difficult by the fact that you thought you were done climbing. As the road ascends around one hairpin turn after another, you settle back in the saddle, put your head down, and resume your cadence with increasingly heavy legs.

∞∞∞

EIGHT

The Long Way Home

WESTMONT COLLEGE RANKS high in the echelon of Christian colleges and universities. Its tuition is the highest among members of the CCCU, an indicator not only of the quality education it provides but also of the need to pay salaries sufficient to attract good faculty and staff to such a costly region. Westmont sometimes is referred to as the Wheaton of the West Coast, and many similarities exist between the two nationally ranked liberal arts colleges.

Following a familiar story line for evangelical higher education, Westmont was founded as the Bible Missionary Institute in 1937 in Los Angeles by Ruth Kerr, owner and CEO of the Kerr Glass Manufacturing Company (maker of those Kerr canning jars in your grandmother's basement). After a few years, the college's leaders decided that the institution should become a Christian liberal arts college, and its name was changed to Westmont College. In 1945, the college moved to a 125-acre estate in Montecito, a wealthy community nestled in the foothills above Santa Barbara. In some way that I as a Midwesterner have yet to figure out, the campus's live oaks, Italian stone pines, and other beautiful trees subsist on ocean mist and a few gulps of rain each year, and as a result, Westmont's campus has a lush garden feel to it despite the arid climate.

Coming from Dutch West Michigan, where tidiness is a religion, I could not help but be struck by both the beautiful setting of the campus and also a certain scruffiness, which I soon realized is typical of California. Students sometimes jokingly call the school "Camp Westmont," and it does exude a bit of summer camp feel, especially the music buildings on the lower campus, which were formerly the Deane School for Boys. Apparently, before the most recent wildfire swept through the campus, bamboo had sprouted up throughout much of the campus, making it difficult to navigate. Even without the bamboo, newcomers to campus typically find themselves wandering down dirt paths, behind buildings, or over stone bridges in an attempt to find their way from one part of campus to another. Fortunately, the college is also built on the side of a mountain, so the two orienting directions are uphill and downhill. One by-product of being located in a community with neighbors such as Oprah Winfrey and Harry and Meghan is a high level of regulation of the campus, including a cap on the number of public events held annually. If one were ranking the bottom ten party campuses in the United States, Westmont would probably challenge for a spot on the list. Furthermore, because the mega-rich apparently enjoy the beauty of the night sky, Westmont's campus is best navigated at night with a flashlight.

What Westmont might lack in nightlife, however, it makes up for in quality academics, as the college excels in providing the traditional college experience. Its 1,200 full-time, residential undergraduate students are taught by nearly one hundred full-time professors; part-time adjuncts are the exception. Classes average under twenty students, and the college generally attracts bright and earnest recruits. Even though few students actually major in music, the college boasts a fifty-member orchestra consisting primarily of non–music majors who nevertheless want to continue playing their instrument in college. In summer 2022, the college switched to a new textbook supply company. Such businesses base their inventory on the average rates of students who actually purchase books for their classes (the number is depressingly low). Unfortunately, the vendor's analytics didn't take into account Westmont students, resulting in a book shortage during its first semester with the college.

True to its traditional nature, Westmont has sought to retain its liberal arts emphasis in a society that increasingly views higher education as a career-preparation service. The college maintains a robust general education program, and the faculty pride themselves on the interdisciplinary nature of their teaching and programs. Participation in study abroad is high, and double majors are common. Nevertheless, the pragmatic trends in higher education have impacted Westmont as well. The two largest majors are business and kinesiology. In 2020, the college started a new major in engineering. More recently, the college launched an accelerated bachelor's degree in nursing program in its new building in downtown Santa Barbara.

And that's where I figured into the equation. One other feature of Westmont's location in one of America's wealthiest communities is "the cap"—a limit of 1,200 on-campus students imposed on the college by the city of Montecito. The cap has helped Westmont maintain its focus on traditional, residential liberal arts education. The problem is, the cost of doing business in higher education continues to rise, reflecting increasing expenses for health care and technology as well as rising customer expectations regarding food, living conditions, and athletic facilities. With tuition already near $50,000 per year, Westmont cannot simply keep raising its price indefinitely, but unlike other colleges, it cannot increase revenue simply by enrolling more students on campus. Thus, if enrollment is going to increase, it must occur off-campus—either in semester-abroad programs that off-load full-time students overseas for a term, or in new programs elsewhere. The nursing major was intended to be the first of several new programs that would enable the college to expand enrollment and increase revenue while maintaining the on-campus cap.

With my background in administration and work with Academ, I came to Westmont partly to oversee innovation and new program development on campus and to help grow "Westmont Downtown," four miles away in Santa Barbara. Ironically, at previous institutions I had always been known as the traditionalist champion of the liberal arts; now I was perceived as the "innovation guy" on campus, and by implication, a potential threat to the college's liberal arts focus. Starting out, therefore, much of my time was spent simply tilling the campus soil for innovation—meeting with professors to listen to their perspectives, assuring faculty that I understood and valued the liberal arts, and fostering conversations about appropriate innovation for a liberal arts college.

For a variety of reasons, however, my role at Westmont didn't materialize as expected. Regarding Westmont Downtown, for example, such developments depended not only on adequate funding and the college's internal approval process, but also on working with the City of Santa Barbara, which has a well-deserved reputation for wearing down new initiatives with bureaucratic inertia. Also, my assigned focus on Downtown resulted in a general sense of isolation from the main campus community, which is what attracted me to the college in the first place. Meanwhile, Lonnie, in her new role as collaborative pianist and choir conductor, soon became a fixture of the Music Department. Students sought her out as their accompanist due to her sight-reading abilities and relational skills, and as accompanist for the Westmont Chamber Singers, she renewed her role as counselor to high-achieving, stressed-out college students. While I took satisfaction in seeing her thrive professionally at Westmont, I felt more like an NFL backup quarterback—a skilled, experienced professional throwing practice balls to wide receivers in pregame warm-ups.

ooooo

If there's a consistent theme throughout my journey in academia, it's that new opportunities materialize, often in unexpected places. Back in 2017, while serving as vice president at the CCCU, I became aware of something new in Christian higher education called a Christian study center. This was a Christian academic community committed to integrating faith and learning, but doing so within the environs of a secular university. In other words, Christian study centers sought to combine the best of two educational worlds—the sense of Christian community and faith integration found at a Christian college, and the significant resources and cultural influence of a major university.

The first study center, and a pattern for the others, was the University of Virginia Study Center in Charlottesville, just a hundred miles south of Washington, DC. The center's director, Drew Trotter, invited me down for a visit. He showed me around the center's two-story building adjacent to campus, which housed a library, offices for staff members and other campus ministries, and ample space for study and interaction among students and faculty. Strolling around the historic campus, Drew and I discussed the remarkable growth of Christian study centers at many of the nation's best universities. Naturally, I asked why there was no Christian study center at the University of Michigan, which consistently ranks as America's top public university. Drew remarked that some initial attempts had been made, but as of yet, Michigan remained one of the top targets for a new Christian study center.

During my three decades in Christian higher education, I never lost my devotion to my alma mater, where my love of academia had been kindled. While at Cornerstone University, I was a member of the University of Michigan chapter of the Fulbright Association. One day each fall, Lonnie, Anna (in high school at the time), and I would drive to Ann Arbor to attend a welcome reception for international students—some of the best and brightest from around the world—who were attending Michigan on Fulbright Scholarships. I also retained an unhealthy emotional connection to Michigan sports, so much so that I often recorded football and basketball games and only watched them after I learned the result, unable to bear the stress of watching the game live. Furthermore, after her COVID-interrupted year in Uganda, Anna attended Michigan's School for Environment and Sustainability to earn a master's degree, which brought Lonnie and me back into Michigan's orbit in a new way.

In February of 2020, amid my consulting work, I visited John Terrill, executive director of an impressive Christian study center at the University of Wisconsin, and we discussed possibilities at Michigan. Soon thereafter, funding materialized from the John Templeton Foundation to enable me to conduct a feasibility study regarding a University of Michigan center. Over the next year, therefore, I added the Michigan project to my other consulting work. I talked with other Christian study center directors and visited Ann Arbor periodically to meet with professors, pastors, and others who had attempted to foster Christian learning at the university. While some modest successes had been achieved, in general the results were disappointing. As one local pastor remarked to me, "Michigan's a tough place for Christians." Thus, in the spring of 2021, while I was in conversation with Westmont about a position there, Lonnie and I were also contemplating a move to Ann Arbor to establish a Christian study center. After my feasibility study, however, it was clear that doing so was premature.

By 2022, the situation had begun to change. Former Taylor University president and Michigan alum Gene Habecker, through an unusual series of events, came into contact with Karl Johnson, the director of the Consortium of Christian Study Centers. Gene was connected to other Michigan alums, and soon a nucleus of support for a Christian study center was developing. At around the same time, Josh Welch, an assistant professor at the University of Michigan School of Medicine, approached Bart Bryant, pastor of Redeemer Ann Arbor, about starting a Christian study center in Redeemer's building, which was situated a half block from the main campus. Redeemer was planning to move to a larger building farther from campus. Rather than sell the church outright, Bart desired to see Redeemer's 150-year-old brick edifice, an Ann Arbor historical landmark, become the incubator for a new Christian study center.

Josh also reached out to Karl Johnson to enlist the Consortium's support of the new venture. Karl thus served as the crucial link between efforts on the ground in Ann Arbor and higher-education professionals such as Gene and myself who were vitally interested in the prospect of a Christian study center at their alma mater. By the summer of 2022, the pieces were finally coming together for a Michigan Christian Study Center. Josh and Bart repurposed Redeemer's building for use as a study center, and Josh lined up a series of Christian faculty speakers on various topics for the fall semester. Meanwhile, we assembled a steering committee that combined Ann Arbor locals and Michigan alums across the United States.

The key ingredients for a Christian study center were developing quickly, with one important gap—a director to oversee the fledgling enterprise and expand its support network. Leading a Christian study center requires an unusual skill set. Because a Christian study center is at heart an academic institution, the director must be an academician who can engage with university faculty and administrators as a peer. Furthermore, because a center is a start-up enterprise, the director must also be an entrepreneur and salesperson who likes to create new things and is comfortable with risk and uncertainty. Also, because typically staffing is limited in a center's early stages, a director should be a jack-of-all-trades who is as comfortable overseeing a building renovation as he or she is hosting a colloquium on faith and science. Finally, because a Christian study center is embedded in a particular university and committed to the flourishing of that institution, a director ideally is an alum who harbors a deep affection for his or her alma mater. The steering committee didn't have to look very far for a candidate who checked all the boxes.

Personal factors were turning our attention back toward Michigan as well. After graduating with her master's degree, Anna became engaged to an Ann Arbor resident (and fellow Michigan alum), had a baby, and settled in the area. After selling our house in East Grand Rapids, we had decided against trying to buy a million-dollar starter home in Santa Barbara. Instead, concluding that Ann Arbor was a solid real estate market, we had reinvested our equity in a house on Ann Arbor's historic Old West Side, which we soon rented out to three medical students. Thus, if we were ever to end up in Ann Arbor, we had the perfect house in which to live: our own.

By March 2023, therefore, we reached another crucial decision point similar to the one four years earlier, when I had to decide between a stable provost role and the riskier path of independent consulting. My role at Westmont was poised to expand, which would necessitate a longer-term commitment, but the rapid development of the Michigan Christian Study Center consumed more of my attention and required on-site leadership. As the new enterprise grew, I began to feel like an absentee parent, missing out on the most important stages in a child's development. Conventional wisdom seemed to suggest that we keep secure, well-paying jobs and stay at Westmont. We could continue for another year or two with a dependable income while helping to develop the Christian Study Center from a distance. Perhaps we were getting too old for leaps into the unknown.

After church one Sunday, however, Lonnie looked at me and reminded me of Kathy Gathro's words on their balcony in March 2019: "Of the options, which one gets you most excited?" Lonnie said, "If the Christian Study Center is where your heart is, what are we waiting for? You're fifty-seven years old and not getting any younger—and since when do we let money dictate our decisions in life?"

It was a wet, dreary day like many others that winter in Santa Barbara, and rather than get my beloved road bike dirty, I took an afternoon run up to Rocky Nook park. Mission Creek, which normally trickles through the park, had been transformed by the rains into a chattering, bubbling torrent. As I sat on a rock by the water, I pulled out my phone and scrolled through my Notes folder, in which various quotes and excerpts had accumulated over the years. My eye fell on a prayer by Desmond Tutu sent to me years earlier by Anna:

> Disturb us, O Lord, when we are too well-pleased with ourselves, when our dreams have come true because we dreamed too little, because we sailed too close to the shore.
>
> Disturb us, O Lord, when with the abundance of things we possess, we have lost our thirst for the water of life, when, having fallen in love with time, we have ceased to dream of eternity.
>
> Stir us, O Lord, to dare more boldly, to venture into wider seas, where storms show Thy mastery, where losing sight of land, we shall find the stars.
>
> In the name of Him who pushed back the horizons of our hopes and invited the brave to follow.
>
> Amen.

I texted Tutu's words to Lonnie, who was talking with Anna on the phone at the time. Two more weeks of deliberations followed—

including confirming that Acadeum would provide me with a part-time salary to work for them from Ann Arbor—but our decision to move to Michigan was basically sealed on that rock by Mission Creek.

ooooo

And so this winding narrative throughout Christian higher education comes full circle to the University of Michigan. The unusual toolbox of skills and experiences that I accumulated over three decades of graduate school, Christian universities, the CCCU, Acadeum, and independent consulting actually equipped me to develop a new form of Christian higher education at my alma mater. When I walk the Michigan campus today, I remember fondly my undergraduate years, and I envision ways that the university can be even better through the influence of a vibrant Christian study center. In an academic culture characterized by polarization and shouting across political divides, Christians can model respectful dialogue, even between those with deep disagreements, because discussion and debate are foundational to truth seeking. In addition, Christian study centers call members of a university community back to an appreciation for teaching, learning, creative work, and scholarship as intrinsic goods that glorify the Creator of all truth. Finally, in the frenetic, performance-based culture of the modern research university, Christians can model a lifestyle that balances the quest for achievement with the virtues of rest and gratitude.

While moving to California seems like a rather roundabout path to get from Grand Rapids to Ann Arbor, in retrospect, Westmont College provided a good position at a first-rate academic institution (and some unforgettable road biking) while the components for a Michigan Christian Study Center gradually developed. My one and only accomplishment as a cook is homemade pizza. In making pizza from scratch, there's a point in the process in which one just has to go find something else to do while the yeast slowly leavens the dough. Westmont provided me with meaningful work while the Christian study center dough was rising, and in fostering greater openness to innovation and starting some new programs,

I was able to make a positive impact while I was there. There's a traditional Wesleyan Covenant Prayer that includes the line, "Let me be employed by thee or laid aside by thee." I've always liked the "let me be employed by thee" part but haven't cared for the "laid aside by thee" part. In retrospect, however, the seemingly "laid aside" times were when I developed many of the skills that I'm using now, and also had the ability to invest in fanning the flame of a new Christian study center.

The months after leaving the CCCU were often scary and difficult, but they also taught me to be entrepreneurial, allowed me to hone some salesmanship skills, and made me more comfortable with risk, confident that God faithfully provides. Ironically, those are the very traits that I draw on at Michigan. Moreover, having joined the "Confederacy of the Humbled" during my landscaping days, the fact that the total annual budget of the Michigan Christian Study Center is a small fraction of the budget of the university that I once led as provost doesn't bother me. After all, the fun lies in building something from scratch.

Will leading the Michigan Christian Study Center conclude my academic journey? It sure seems like it. But I'm hanging on to my paint brushes and leaf rake just in case.

EPILOGUE

A Second-Mountain College

I HAVE SPENT THREE DECADES in academia, have visited nearly one hundred campuses, and have made a concerted effort these past few years to keep academic leaders informed about the state of Christian higher education. I'm sometimes asked, therefore, for my advice regarding the future of the movement. Have I discovered any silver bullet that will help Christian colleges weather the current storms and thrive in the future? Unfortunately I have not, but I do have some thoughts on the subject nonetheless.

Needless to say, the big picture seems daunting. Carleton College economist Nathan Grawe has become the go-to downer at academic conferences in describing the demographic realities of fewer high school graduates, especially in the Midwest and Northeast (which, of course, also happen to be the regions with the highest density of colleges and universities). In *The Agile College: How Institutions Successfully Navigate Demographic Change*, Grawe argues that low US fertility rates over the past decade will result in a significant decline in the number of potential college students by the mid-2020s. While these trends have already impacted the Midwest and Northeast, they will affect other areas as well. Thus, colleges will continue to grapple with declining enrollments and the ripple effects on campus budgets and infrastructure.[20]

In August 2022, the *Chronicle of Higher Education* ran a feature article, "The Shrinking of Higher Education," which noted that in spring 2022, enrollment at colleges and universities nationwide was down 7.4 percent from spring 2020, and demographic trends continue to look ominous for the future. Moreover, surveys indicate that public confidence in higher education is declining, and employers demonstrate an increasing openness to hiring employees without a college degree. Not to be outdone, that same month, *Inside Higher Ed* featured a piece by Temple University president Jason Wingard entitled "Higher Ed Must Change or Die," which reinforced these alarming trends. It's no wonder that a veteran provost once remarked to me over a pint at an academic conference, "We're all just in the business of managing decline."[21]

Given these realities, some have predicted, or even called for, a culling of the herd to reduce the number of colleges competing for a shrinking pool of students. And while a few schools do close their doors each year, some observers seem to overlook the differences between colleges and other service providers. Unlike hospitals, colleges represent shared communities existing over decades or centuries, united by emotional ties to a place and an experience. If I were to have knee surgery at St. Mary's Hospital, I wouldn't wear a St. Mary's sweatshirt to demonstrate my continued loyalty. Simply shuttering a college is not as simple as it may seem.

Nevertheless, it may well be time for some colleges to consider the external realities and conclude that it's time to call it a day. Perhaps for some institutions, wise leadership means focusing not on survival at all costs but on ending well, being grateful for the legacy that will continue in its graduates, and trusting that the global movement of Christian higher education will continue flowing in other streams. In doing so, they might benefit their peers by freeing up potential students. Before I arrived at Cornerstone University, it had absorbed the struggling Grand Rapids School of Bible and Music, and for that institution, such an acquisition was an honorable end to decades of operation.

The vast majority of Christian colleges and universities, of course, will continue sailing on into brisk headwinds. But how? When I was transitioning out of the CCCU, the more I scanned the horizon wondering what was out there, the scarier my situation appeared. When I focused on the particular day, and whatever green light was in front of me, my situation seemed less daunting and more manageable. Likewise, when colleges focus on the task at hand and consider what resources are at their disposal, their situations may seem less dire.

For one thing, broad demographic trends are too blunt of an instrument to apply to particular institutional contexts. Consider the following: In 2019, there were nearly 20 million full-time college students in the United States. About three-quarters of them attended public universities, leaving all the private institutions to fight over 5 million students. Imagine what even a 2 percent shift in attendance from public to private institutions could mean for the potential student pool for Christian colleges and universities. Moreover, because most students attend a college in their region, national trends are not the entire story for most institutions. Competition tends to be local. The antelope doesn't have to outrun the cheetah; it just needs to outrun one other antelope. Applied to Christian higher education, that means that John Brown University doesn't have to outcompete Brown University; it just needs to run faster than a few other regional options that its prospective students are considering.

So what does it mean to run faster than one's counterparts in the competitive, crowded world of US higher education? Christian colleges and universities need to look more deeply than programs and buildings to understand their core value. For such institutions, their primary asset is not high-tech classrooms, gourmet food, stimulating chapel speakers, or trendy majors. It's their ability to provide students not just with what students *think* they're looking for—preparation for a successful career—but with what we as Christians know they're *really* looking for: authentic community.

In *The Life We're Looking For: Reclaiming Relationship in a Technological World*, Andy Crouch observes that the most basic human need is to be known. We are wired for embodied, dependent relationships with other humans and cannot fully develop as humans without such community. Writes Crouch, "Only when we know and are known by others can we become fully ourselves."[22] Throughout history, however, humans have sought to insulate themselves from relationships and to control nature and other humans. The features of our technological age, such as digital devices and social media, amplify this age-old tendency and give us ever more effective tools to attempt to control our environment and to create simulated rather than real community.

Crouch identifies the deeper threat in our technological age as what Jesus called "Mammon"—a force at work in the world throughout history that seeks to treat humans as objects for economic gain. Crouch writes, "God wishes to bring forth the flourishing of creation through the flourishing of persons. Mammon wants to put all persons into the service of things and ultimately to bring about the exploitation of all of creation."[23] Or to put it differently, our core problem isn't that we're hooked on iPhones and our attention is being co-opted by algorithm-based advertising. It's that we inhabit a technological society that fundamentally tilts away from the qualities of community, embodiment, and presence that make us human and give us fulfillment. That's why sociologists today often point to loneliness as the quintessentially modern epidemic.

Christian institutions, however, can provide a compelling alternative. At its inception, Christianity asserted a countercultural way of life in which people were valued as real persons who formed authentic communities, even across the traditional social boundary lines of male and female, Jew and non-Jew, slave and free. Concerning Christian higher education, therefore, while there's no secret formula that will magically produce success, if Christian colleges and universities have any edge on the competition, it's this: because of their rootedness in Christian truth, such institutions have the opportunity to create authentic communities that are most attuned to the basic desires of the human soul. As David Brooks wrote in *The Social Animal*, "Your unconsciousness wants to entangle you in the thick web of relations that are the essence of human flourishing."[24] In fact, the remarkable growth of the Christian study center movement stems in large part from the ability of such centers to create vibrant communities where students and faculty find a sense of belonging within a large and in some cases impersonal public university. For Christian colleges and universities, the key to institutional flourishing, I would suggest, is not one single thing, but a variety of features united by the common theme of providing students, faculty, and staff with the ability to be truly known.

Fortunately, authentic community is not just a Christian add-on to university life, but is an important contributor to quality education as well. Robert Detweiler, in *The Evidence Liberal Arts Needs*, surveyed graduates of US universities to ascertain the key features of undergraduate education that yield the most successful long-term results. The most important factors, he concludes, are a course of study that spans a broad range of subjects, engaging pedagogy, and most importantly, "relational learning"—that is, a sense of authentic community characterized by meaningful relationships between professors and students.[25] So if authentic community is crucial both for human flourishing and for quality academics, how might Christian colleges capitalize on that insight?

First, colleges may need to invert the approach to undergraduate education that many institutions take—that of starting with the student's major and building out around it. Resource-challenged colleges often assign lower-level general education courses to adjunct professors or create introductory "supercourses" of hundreds of students so that they can devote their primary institutional resource—full-time professors—to upper-level major courses. But if students form communities early in their college experience (or don't form them at all), and academic mentoring is truly important, it makes more sense to invest full-time professors in those lower-level general education courses that are formative to students' academic and personal growth, and to keep those courses to a manageable size. Moreover, it's more likely to be upper-level specialized courses, not general education, that benefit from adjunct professors who are active in the professional world.

Of course, shifting the educational model from preparation in majors to formation in community means hiring professors who are primarily committed to engaging with students and developing mentoring relationships with them, both inside and outside the classroom. Christian colleges and universities have done much to overcome Mark Noll's "scandal of the evangelical mind" in the past two decades, and they should continue to hire and support Christian scholars. But a key concern in the hiring process must also be identifying professors who are also committed to the formation of their students. It doesn't have to be one or the other. The best scholars in my university experiences—John Walton and George Marsden—were also my most formative mentors.

Envisioning the Christian college primarily as authentic community, with student-faculty relationships and small, engaging classes as central to the enterprise, doesn't obviate the need to offer attractive majors. It might, however, lead colleges to reframe their approach to recruiting students, recognizing that quality community is ultimately what will attract them. We can think of a high-demand major such as engineering, for example, not necessarily as a hook to snag the fish; the "hook" is the strength of the college community. Rather, engineering is the net that the angler places under the fish when it's being brought into the boat so that it doesn't wriggle off the hook and fall back into the water. In other words, the greatest value of a market-driven major might be to get students' attention in the first place, and then preventing them from enrolling elsewhere because of that major's absence.

Moreover, colleges that establish authentic community as their core can be more nimble around the margins in order to develop such attractive majors. As *Good to Great* author Gary Collins famously advised: "First who, then what." A stable foundation rooted in full-time faculty mentors, quality teaching, and strong student development programs makes possible a periphery of market-oriented programs that can fluctuate as conditions change. Many colleges' decision-making structures are relics of an era when institutional stability was the primary value and are thus designed to slow down innovation and maintain the status quo. College leaders may need to revise existing systems or develop new ones that allow for more adaptability around a stable academic and communal core. Faculty and administrators should see themselves not as members of a symphony diligently playing their rehearsed notes, but rather as jazz musicians improvising on a few chord charts. When I was leaving the CCCU, I found my way to a new career by following the green lights that appeared and by staying in motion. Each university will also have to be willing to adapt to changing conditions, and perhaps at times stumble its way to new approaches that are right for it.

If the chief asset of a Christian college is authentic community, it can also benefit by extending that sense of belonging to students beyond graduation. In other words, a thriving Christian institution will view students as clients who engage in the academic community in various ways throughout their lives. In *College Unbound: The Future of Higher Education and What It Means for Students*, Jay Selingo argues that the educational wave of the future will consist of students assembling for themselves a meaningful education from a variety of different institutions and experiences. Just as music-streaming technology puts individual consumers in the driver's seat and enables them to assemble a playlist from multiple artists, Selingo claims, so digital education will empower students to select only those educational experiences that they need to prepare for their chosen career pathway.[26]

The problem with such an analogy, however, is that most of us don't want to have to assemble all of our own playlists, nor are we very good at doing so. If left to ourselves, we would simply replay the same old songs (case in point: my biking playlist, consisting primarily of angry screamer-band tunes, was assembled for me by my oldest son over a decade ago). We long to be members of communities that can expose us to new songs and, dare I suggest, provide us with *experts* who can teach us to discriminate between good and bad music. A more authentically human approach to education, as described in Chris Gallagher's *College Made Whole: Integrative Learning for a Divided World*, is for institutions to view their students as lifelong clients in the learning process, whose need for education in our fast-changing society will continue throughout their lives.[27] A wise, discerning use of online education, for example, can enable colleges to cultivate learning communities across the generations, yielding both educational and financial benefits.

Reconceiving a college's prime value as providing a vibrant learning community entails a risk: its value is not as readily apparent to outside observers as a new media center or an indoor climbing wall. Roosevelt Montas, in his book *Rescuing Socrates: How the Great Books Changed My Life and Why They Matter for a New Generation*, likens explaining the value of the liberal arts to explaining the plot of a great novel: "The value of the thing cannot be extracted and delivered apart from the thing itself. . . . Contagion is the only way to transmit its value."[28] His insight would seem to apply to authentic community as well, especially in a modern society in which true community seems increasingly rare.

That's why, to return to an earlier theme, sales is important in academia. When I was a young professor, I assumed that it was Admissions' job to fill my classroom with students; my job was to teach them. That was naive then, and it's unrealistic in today's environment. Professors are colleges' most valuable assets, and they would do well to put aside any academic scruples about "sales" and enthusiastically promote the value of their school to prospective students and parents. Christian colleges need to develop a shared language to describe their value and ensure that everyone, from the grounds crew to the president, embraces their roles as spokespersons for a campus rooted in authentic community.

∞∞∞

Of course, creating academic communities in which each member knows and is known by others has implications for size. Human-centered education cannot be scaled up infinitely because a skilled professor can only teach and mentor a finite number of students, and Student Life staff members can only invest in the lives of so many individuals. Wendell Berry, in his essay "A Good Farmer of the Old School," describes a dairy farmer named Lancie who claimed that a farmer could only manage well about twenty-five cows. "If a fellow milks twenty-five cows," Lancie says, "he'll *see* them all." More than that, and he might touch them all but he won't *see* them all. And that number has implications not only for the cows but also for the financial health of the farm. Beyond twenty-five, Lancie remarks, "You're overlooking things that cost you money." I wouldn't want to push the analogy between students and dairy cows too far, but

Berry's insights have important implications for Christian colleges. Human-centered education—education that is as much *cultivation* as instruction—can only be done well at a scale in which professors, students, and staff members can know and interact with each other personally. Like a roller-coaster ride, formative education takes place in groups small enough to fit into the actual cars that career around the tracks. As Berry aptly concludes, "proper scale permits a correct balance between work and care."[29]

Ultimately, then, for Christian colleges and universities to thrive in the future as communities that balance work and care, they may have to adjust their understanding of what it means to be "sustainable." Colleges and universities operate in a capitalist society that historically has been predicated on continual growth. Now that the effects of human activity on the environment seem apparent, we are recognizing that continual growth is neither possible nor desirable. Modern society is struggling to come to terms with a new social and economic order in which expansion and ever-increasing productivity are replaced by balance and appropriate limitations. Perhaps it's time to apply such thinking to our institutions as well and replace a "grow or die" mentality with a new paradigm.

As individuals, we are called to contentment, to disciplined living within our means. Continually chasing a bigger house, a higher salary, and more stuff is a sign of spiritual immaturity, not wisdom. Perhaps Christian colleges and universities can adopt a similar mind-set. Doing so would require that we learn to see our primary value not in the new things that we initiate but in the healthy communities that we cultivate and the daily activities that take place on our campuses. While that might sound like a simple change, it may be quite radical. Imagine a college president going to a board meeting not with a list of new programs launched or the latest building project, but with a compilation of how many students visited professors in their offices, how many classes under twenty-five students the college offered, or how many non–music majors performed in the university's musical production.

That's not to say that we no longer seek change or innovation. As I have suggested, the Christian college with a strong communal core can become more adaptable, not less, in its peripheral programs and offerings. But as Wendell Berry writes, "Once we grant the possibility of a proper human scale, . . . we realize that we are less interested in technological 'breakthroughs' than in technological elegance. Of a new tool or method we will no longer ask, Is it fast? Is it powerful? . . . We will ask instead, Is it fitting to our real needs? Is it becoming to us? Is it unhealthy or ugly?" Berry concludes, "Though we may keep a certain interest in innovation and in what we may become, we will also renew our interest in what we have been."[30] Christian colleges that prioritize the human scale will foster innovations that enable them to be healthier, more thriving communities, not simply ones that promise continual expansion.

To adjust our mind-set toward "human-scaled" universities, it might be helpful to distinguish between intrinsic and instrumental goods. Intrinsic goods are things that are good for their own sake, regardless of what other benefits they produce. Good health, a beautiful sunset, and a great work of art are intrinsic goods, regardless of what other practical benefits they might produce. From a Christian perspective, the daily life of a college campus, like a Beethoven symphony, is full of all sorts of intrinsic goods. A student paying attention to a lecture and learning the skill of taking concise notes is intrinsically good, as is a professor grading a paper and providing constructive feedback, a resident director meeting a student for coffee, and a violinist giving a lesson. Perhaps the more that we recognize and celebrate these intrinsic goods, the more content we can be with our institutions as they currently exist, rather than how we wish them to be.

Fortunately, these intrinsic goods tend to produce instrumental goods as well. In fact, as Robert Detweiler shows in *The Evidence Liberal Arts Needs*, the human-scaled, formative experiences that colleges and universities provide also produce graduates who are more likely to lead successful, productive, and fulfilling lives. We can trumpet such instrumental benefits and promote our statistics regarding career placements and *U.S. News and World Report* rankings, but we should avoid equating those features as the ultimate indicators of our worth as institutions.

ooooo

Twenty-seven years ago, I emerged from Notre Dame, PhD in hand, ready to take on the academic world. A $28,000 starting salary at Grand Canyon University wasn't a lot, but it was a foothold in professional academia. From there, I climbed the academic ladder for two decades, and it was easy to assume that progress toward bigger and better things was the Christian's inevitable calling. Eventually—in the fall of 2018, to be exact—I discovered otherwise. God calls us to faithfulness, not to progress, and the direction of that calling might be upward or downward, at least from a secular perspective. Through no plan of my own, I became what David Brooks calls a "Second-Mountain" person for whom the quest for professional success is overshadowed by devotion to deeper qualities of faithfulness, community, and meaningful service.[31]

What would it mean for Christian colleges and universities to become Second-Mountain institutions, less concerned with achievement and outward success and more devoted to becoming the sorts of academic communities in which individuals know and are known by others, colleges that perhaps do not increase in size or resources but grow in faithfulness to their calling? Such institutions need to be wise and market-savvy, of course. But in a broader perspective, being market-savvy means understanding what kind of life students *as human beings* desire and organizing themselves accordingly. Doing so might be not only their competitive advantage in the contested terrain of higher education, but also their deeper contribution to the common good in a troubled world.

For Further Reading

NEEDLESS TO SAY, books abound on higher education in general, and on Christian higher education in particular. Any professional who has read widely in the field will have a unique list of recommendations that reflects his or her own particular interests and experiences. What follows, therefore, is by no means exhaustive, but rather a sampling of helpful texts from the past few decades that reflect my own idiosyncratic tastes.

SOME FOUNDATIONAL WORKS

George Marsden, *The Soul of the American University Revisited: From Protestant to Postsecular* (Oxford: Oxford University Press, 2021). This is an updated version of Marsden's classic 1996 book, which traces the general trajectory of mainstream higher education in the United States from sectarian Protestant to pervasively secular. Marsden's book provides the basic foundation for understanding modern American higher education, Christian or otherwise.

William Ringenberg, *The Christian College: A History of Protestant Higher Education in America* (Grand Rapids: Baker Books, 2006). Ringenberg's subject is a subset of Marsden's; he focuses on the development of private Christian colleges. It lacks Marsden's broad narrative scope but provides helpful information for understanding the historical context of today's Christian colleges.

Mark Noll, *The Scandal of the Evangelical Mind* (Grand Rapids: Eerdmans, 1994). Combining history and jeremiad, Noll's analysis of evangelical anti-intellectualism and his proposed remedies first appeared over twenty-five years ago, but it continues to constitute an important backdrop for Christian colleges and universities.

Charles Cotherman, *To Think Christianly: A History of L'Abri, Regent College, and the Christian Study Center Movement* (Downers Grove, IL: InterVarsity Press, 2020). The Christian Study Center movement is almost too young to have a history, but Cotherman ably traces the historical roots and development of this growing presence on US campuses.

Two general summaries of the purpose of Christian higher education are Arthur Holmes's classic work, *The Idea of a Christian College* (Grand Rapids: Eerdmans, 1975), and, more recently, Rick Ostrander, *Why College Matters to God: An Introduction to Christian Learning* (Abilene, TX: Abilene Christian University Press, 2021).

The Modern Educational Landscape

Clayton M. Christiansen first explored what he called the coming "disruption" of higher education in his classic work *The Innovative University: Changing the DNA of Higher Education from the Inside Out* (Hoboken, NJ: Jossey-Bass, 2011). A more current exposition in the "disruption" vein is Arthur Levine and Scott Van Pelt, *The Great Upheaval: Higher Education's Past, Present, and Uncertain Future* (Baltimore: Johns Hopkins University Press, 2021). More descriptive and less prescriptive is Bryan Alexander's *Academia Next: The Futures of Higher Education* (Baltimore: Johns Hopkins University Press, 2020).

Two recent books analyze the demographic and financial challenges confronting higher education today: Nathan Grawe, *The Agile College: How Institutions Successfully Navigate Demographic Changes* (Baltimore: Johns Hopkins University Press, 2021), and Jon McGee, *Breakpoint: The Changing Marketplace for Higher Education* (Baltimore: Johns Hopkins University Press, 2015).

Jay Selingo's *College Unbound: The Future of Higher Education and What It Means for Students* (Amazon, 2013) argues for the "unbundling" of higher education, which would enable consumers/students to construct their own individualized educational experiences from multiple institutions. In contrast, Chris Gallagher, in *College Made Whole: Integrative Learning for a Divided World* (Baltimore: Johns Hopkins University Press, 2019), argues that colleges' futures lie in providing continuous, integrative learning communities that persist throughout adult life for their graduates.

Two recent books provide compelling arguments for liberal arts education in a society that increasingly seems to view higher education as synonymous with career preparation: Richard Detweiler, *The Evidence Liberal Arts Needs: Lives of Consequence, Inquiry, and Accomplishment* (Cambridge, MA: MIT Press, 2021), and Roosevelt Montas, *Rescuing Socrates: How the Great Books Changed My Life and Why They Matter for a New Generation* (Princeton, NJ: Princeton University Press, 2021).

ACADEMIC LEADERSHIP

To borrow from an ancient author, "Of the writing of books on leadership, there is no end." Three books in particular—and by no means the most recent—have been most helpful to me: Lee Bolman and Joan Gallos, *Reframing Academic Leadership* (Hoboken, NJ: Jossey-Bass, 2011), is a comprehensive how-to manual on the basic principles and methods of organizational leadership in an academic setting. Steven Sample's *The Contrarian's Guide to Leadership* (Hoboken, NJ: Jossey-Bass, 2002) has been around for two decades, but it continues to be practical and combines a wealth of examples from the world of a university president. Bill Robinson's *Incarnate Leadership: Five Leadership Lessons from the Life of Jesus* (Grand Rapids: Zondervan, 2009) is a simple, concise pastoral guide to leadership based on the experiences of a Christian college president.

THEOLOGICAL CONTEXT FOR CHRISTIAN HIGHER EDUCATION

James Davison Hunter's *To Change the World: The Irony, Tragedy, and Possibility of Christianity in the Late Modern World* (Oxford: Oxford University Press, 2010) is a classic sociological treatment of the role of Christianity in secular society. His prescription of a "faithful presence" provides a theological foundation for the work of Christian universities and Christian study centers.

The works of Calvin University philosophy professor James K. A. Smith, in which he explores the formative influences of "cultural liturgies," are essential reading for anyone involved in Christian worship, formation, or pedagogy. Perhaps the most relevant for Christian colleges is the first: *Desiring the Kingdom: Worship, Worldview, and Cultural Formation* (Grand Rapids: Baker Academic, 2009).

More recently, Andy Crouch's *The Life We're Looking For: Reclaiming Relationship in a Technological World* (New York: Convergent, 2022) emphasizes the importance of physical-based human communities, and by extension, the opportunity for Christian institutions to fill a void in modern society.

CHRISTIAN HIGHER EDUCATION DISTINCTIVES

Models for Christian Higher Education: Strategies for Success (Grand Rapids: Eerdmans, 1997), edited by Richard Hughes and William

Adrian, categorizes approaches to Christian higher education by various faith traditions that are still relevant and useful today. Similarly, Nicholas Wolterstorff's *Educating for Shalom: Essays on Christian Higher Education* (Grand Rapids: Eerdmans, 2004) is a timeless classic on the purposes of Christian higher education whose themes have been discussed and extended over the past two decades.

Two of the leading current thinkers on Christian higher education are Perry Glanzer and David Smith. Among their many works are *Restoring the Soul of the University: Unifying Christian Higher Education in a Fragmented Age* (Downers Grove, IL: InterVarsity Press, 2017), by Perry Glanzer, Nathan Alleman, and Todd Ream; and *On Christian Teaching: Practicing Faith in the Classroom* (Grand Rapids: Eerdmans, 2018), by David Smith.

Periodicals and Blogs

In addition to books, those wishing to stay informed on US higher education would do well to consult periodicals and blogs that provide weekly or daily updates on events in the field. The two standard sources of information for higher education in general are the *Chronicle of Higher Education* and *Inside Higher Education*. In addition, two sources provide daily insight and commentary on topics in Christian higher education: *Christian Scholars' Review* (https://christianscholars.com/blog/) and Bethel University (MN) historian Christopher Gehrz's *The Pietist Schoolman* (https://pietist schoolman.com/blog/).

Notes

1. Virginia Brereton, *Training God's Army: The American Bible School, 1880–1940* (Bloomington: Indiana University Press, 1990).

2. Quoted in George M. Marsden, *Fundamentalism and American Culture: The Shaping of Twentieth-Century Evangelicalism, 1870–1925* (New York: Oxford University Press, 1980), 113.

3. George M. Marsden, *The Soul of the American University: From Protestant Establishment to Established Nonbelief* (New York: Oxford University Press, 1994), 167–80.

4. Marsden, *Fundamentalism and American Culture*.

5. Audrey June, "Oh, the Places They'll Go with a Ph.D.," *Chronicle of Higher Education*, June 27, 2022.

6. Quoted in Mark R. Schwehn, *Exiles from Eden: Religion and the Academic Vocation in America* (New York: Oxford University Press, 1993), ix.

7. Mark A. Noll, *The Scandal of the Evangelical Mind* (Grand Rapids: Eerdmans, 1994), 3.

8. Rick Ostrander, *Head, Heart, and Hand: John Brown University and Modern Evangelical Higher Education* (Fayetteville: University of Arkansas Press, 2003), 33.

9. Ostrander, *Head, Heart, and Hand*, 79.

10. Ann Patchett, *Bel Canto* (New York: HarperCollins, 2001), 165.

11. 2001 CCCU Task Force on Human Sexuality (in CCCU Archives).

12. Cited in "Two CCCU Colleges to Allow Same-Sex Married Faculty," *Christianity Today*, July 28, 2015.

13. "Peace Church Out: Mennonite Schools Leave CCCU to Avoid Same-Sex Marriage Split," *Christianity Today*, September 21, 2015.

14. See "Overview," Council for Christian Colleges & Universities, accessed February 27, 2023, https://www.cccu.org/institutions/#heading -categories-3.

15. Gary Klein, "Performing a Project Pre-Mortem," *Harvard Business Review Magazine*, September 2007.

16. Henri Nouwen, *Seeds of Hope: A Henri Nouwen Reader* (New York: Bantam Books, 1997).

17. Amor Towles, *A Gentleman in Moscow* (New York: Viking Penguin, 2016), 196.

18. Henri Nouwen, *Discernment: Reading the Signs of Daily Life* (San Francisco: HarperOne, 2013), 156, 150.

19. Richard Rohr, *Falling Upward* (San Francisco: Jossey-Bass, 2011), 66.

20. Nathan Grawe, *The Agile College: How Institutions Successfully Navigate Demographic Change* (Baltimore: Johns Hopkins University Press, 2021).

21. Karin Fischer, "The Shrinking of Higher Education," *Chronicle of Higher Education*, August 12, 2022; Jason Wingard, "Higher Ed Must Change or Die," *Inside Higher Ed*, August 16, 2022.

22. Andy Crouch, *The Life We're Looking For: Reclaiming Relationship in a Technological World* (New York: Convergent Books, 2022), 29.

23. Crouch, *The Life We're Looking For*, 78.

24. David Brooks, *The Social Animal: The Hidden Sources of Love, Character, and Achievement* (New York: Random House, 2012), xviii.

25. Robert Detweiler, *The Evidence Liberal Arts Needs: Lives of Consequence, Inquiry, and Achievement* (Cambridge, MA: MIT Press, 2021).

26. Jay Selingo, *College Unbound: The Future of Higher Education and What It Means for Students* (Boston: Houghton Mifflin Harcourt, 2013).

27. Chris Gallagher, *College Made Whole: Integrative Learning for a Divided World* (Baltimore: Johns Hopkins University Press, 2019).

28. Roosevelt Montas, *Rescuing Socrates: How the Great Books Changed My Life and Why They Matter for a New Generation* (Princeton: Princeton University Press, 2021).

29. Wendell Berry, *Home Economics: Fourteen Essays* (Berkeley, CA: Counterpoint, 1987), 154.

30. Wendell Berry, "Getting Along with Nature," in *Home Economics*, 16–17.

31. David Brooks, *The Second Mountain: The Quest for a Moral Life* (New York: Random House, 2019).

Index

Michigan Christian Study Center, 162–65, 166–67
Michigan Colleges Alliance (MCA), 112
Michigan Independent Colleges and Universities (MICU), 112
Miller, Herman, 89
Miller, Walter, 115
Mine Eyes Have Seen the Glory (Balmer), 70
Miscamble, Wilson, 41
missionary service, 9–10; Eastern Europe, 38–39
Models for Christian Higher Education (Hughes and Adrian), 182–83
Mondale, Walter, 4
Montas, Roosevelt, 175, 181
Moody, Dwight L., 2, 8
Moody Bible Institute, 1–2, 82; academics, 13, 15; basketball team, 5–7; Bible courses, 13–14, 16–17; dating during 1980s, 4–5; Founder's Week, 8; missionary kid subculture, 12; missions conference, 9; personal evangelism requirements, 10; practical Christian ministry (PCM), 10–11; spiritual atmosphere, 7–9; student hijinks, 11–12
Moreno-Riano, Gerson, 105–7
Mount St. Joseph University, 150
Mouw, Richard, 35
Muir, Pete, 92
Murray, Charles, 20

Nagel Institute for World Christianity, 142
National Association of Evangelicals, 115
National Association of Independent Colleges & Universities (NAICU), 112
National Christian College Athletic Conference, 5
New Faculty Institute, 122
Noll, Mark, 35, 64–65, 67, 69, 70, 173, 180
Nolt, Steven, 48
NOMA (nonoverlapping magisteria), 33
Northern Illinois University (NIU), 21
Nouwen, Henri, 131–32, 136–37

Obergefell v. Hodges, 115, 116. *See also* same-sex marriage
Oklahoma Wesleyan University, 116
Oliver, Carrie, 74
Oliver, Dub, 116
Oliver, Gary, 74
Oliver, Mary, 121
On Christian Teaching (Smith), 183
O'Neal, Bryan, 14
online education, 147, 174; Academ (course-sharing platform), 147, 148–49, 150, 153, 155; COVID-19 pandemic, 152–53
Orthodox Presbyterian Church (OPC), 44

Index

Westminster Theological Seminary, 44
Westmont College, 73, 151, 154–55, 158–60
Wheaton College, 35, 63, 64, 98, 99, 118
Wheeler, Liz, 91, 107–8
White, Mel, 100
Whitworth University, 119

Why College Matters to God (Ostrander), 31, 81, 93, 180
Wingard, Jason, 169
Wolpoff, Milford, 33
Wolterstorff, Nicholas, 35, 74, 183
Wubbena, Jan Helmut, 61
Wubbena, Terri, 61

Yes We Can Coalition, 112